OXFORD MEDICAL PUBLICATIONS

Handbook of Record Linkage

Handbook of
Record Linkage

Methods for Health and Statistical Studies,
Administration, and Business

HOWARD B. NEWCOMBE

Formerly Head, Population Research Branch,
Atomic Energy of Canada Ltd,
Chalk River Nuclear Laboratories
Ontario

OXFORD   NEW YORK   TOKYO
OXFORD   UNIVERSITY   PRESS
1988

Oxford University Press, Walton Street, Oxford OX2 6DP
Oxford New York Toronto
Delhi Bombay Calcutta Madras Karachi
Petaling Jaya Singapore Hong Kong Tokyo
Nairobi Dar es Salaam Cape Town
Melbourne Auckland
and associated companies in
Berlin Ibadan

Oxford is a trade mark of Oxford University Press

Published in the United States
by Oxford University Press, New York

British Library Cataloguing in Publication Data
Newcombe, Howard B.
Handbook of record linkage: methods for
health and statistical studies, administration
and business.
1. Machine-readable files. Design & management
I. Title.
005.74
ISBN 0-19-261732-X

Library of Congress Cataloging in Publication Data
Newcombe, Howard B.
Handbook of record linkage: methods for health and statistical
studies, administration and business/Howard B. Newcombe.
p. cm.—(Oxford medical publications)
Bibliography: p.   Includes index.
1. Medical record linkage.   2. Business records—Management.
I. Title.   II. Series.
R864.N44   1988   651.5' 04261—dc19   87-34947
ISBN 0-19-261732-X

Set by Colset Private Ltd
Printed in Great Britain
at the University Printing House, Oxford
by David Stanford
Printer to the University

Preface

Record linkage, whether for the purpose of health follow-up and statistics, or for administration and business, is not an activity that an individual investigator can pursue in isolation. The present account therefore owes much to the help of organizations and various collaborations with individuals over a period in excess of 30 years.

The organizations that have sponsored such work and with which I have been personally involved, in one way or another, are numerous. Especially, I would like to recognize here the support given from the mid-1950s by the Chalk River Nuclear Laboratories of Atomic Energy of Canada Limited, during my employment there until 1979. Such endeavours are now being carried on by Statistics Canada, which had necessarily been involved virtually from the beginning and with whom I later served as a consultant. Statistics Canada has moreover contributed in a definitive way to the mathematical theory of record linkage, and has developed an exceedingly flexible computer system for handling all aspects of a linkage operation. Particular mention should be made also of Eldorado Nuclear Limited, later Eldorado Resources Limited, which carried out, under John Abbatt's direction and in collaboration with Statistics Canada and the NCIC (National Cancer Institute of Canada) Epidemiology Unit at the University of Toronto, a cohort study of the mortality experience of their uranium workers and other employees. This provided substantial recent experience in the refinement of the linkage procedures, and I was involved in these refinements as a consultant to Eldorado.

Of those individuals to whom the contents of this handbook owe much, special mention should be made of Martha Elaine Smith and Pierre Lalonde of the Occupational and Environmental Health Unit at Statistics Canada. Miss Smith (now Mrs Fair) did such work for a considerable period at Chalk River before joining Statistics Canada, and Mr Lalonde has actively generated refinements together with much of the currently available information on the consequences of particular linkage procedures. His data have been employed freely in the examples for the present account. The writer is indebted also to Francis Pring-Mill and Ted Hill of Statistics Canada, for their thoughtful and cogent comments on a draft version of this handbook.

Discussions with individuals, particularly where a contentious or elusive technical point is at issue, have often been invaluable. I recall one especially rewarding three-way debate by correspondence with David Binder of Statistics Canada and Geoffrey Howe of the NCIC Epidemiology Unit. None of us had the complete and correct answer at the outset, but the truth emerged through a vigorous process of exchange. May there be more of such in the future, with those who are willing to pursue the logic to a mutually satisfactory conclusion.

Deep River   H.B.N.
November 1987

Contents

Introduction

The present account has been written for those who may become involved in computerized searches of large files of records. It is especially relevant wherever the identifying particulars used for searching and 'linking' the records are prone to change or are less than reliably reported, as is true of names of people and of companies. Even personal identity numbers and account numbers fall into this category wherever occasional numerical errors cause names and such to be employed as back-up. Indeed, virtually all file searches are probabilistic in nature to some degree.

The numbers of people involved in such probabilistic file searching are on the upswing for various reasons. These have to do with health and statistical investigations, and also with administration and business.

In matters of health, increasing public awareness of occupational and environmental risks, especially of cancer, has resulted in frequent demands that suspected effects be investigated. Much of the relevant information about the individuals who may have been harmed is now put routinely into machine-readable form. So it is technically quite possible to follow up the mortality and health experience of very large cohorts that are thought to be at some special risk. Indeed, there is a great deal of experience in the matter already. The procedures may be applied in a similar fashion to statistical studies of the economic indicators of personal well-being, and even to analogous follow-up of businesses to determine the correlates of their successes and failures.

In matters of administration and business, record linkage has applications to revenue, welfare and social security, credit, customer and subscription lists, and other public- and private-sector activities. For these, it is not yet customary to adopt a probabilistic approach, but costly clerical interventions could often be reduced if more advanced procedures were employed, similar to those already developed for health studies.

When large-scale searching is done by a computer it is best that it have a probabilistic basis. But few people have become experienced in the associated logic and practice. Record linkage is not a recognized part of the training of either the programmer or the computer systems specialist, nor of the epidemiologist or the accountant. True, there is in existence a considerable body of relevant mathematical theory, but the publications containing it are written for mathematicians and are apt to be intimidating to others. This is unfortunate because the logic is inherently simple and natural, and it is applied routinely in the mind of any perceptive human searcher who attempts to do the job manually.

The purpose of the present account is therefore to meet the needs of those who may want a guide to linkage practice with which to get started on this unfamiliar task. The intention is that the simplicity of the underlying principle be apparent at all times, that its application be sophisticated enough to get the job done efficiently, and that the mathematics be correctly described in plain language.

Part I

The basics and their application

1

The files and the task

By far the greatest current use of probabilistic record linkage is in health studies, where it is most frequently employed for searches of large files of death records. On a smaller scale, there has been a wide diversity of uses of the linkage procedures. The vital records and a number of special disease registers are linkable with each other and can be searched. Other kinds of records have been variously employed, for example to initiate such searches, to provide additional health information, and to verify that individuals are indeed alive. As well, the linkage methods have been used to purge files of unsuspected duplicate entries. For present purposes, however, what is important is that the procedures and the logic are similar throughout.

To simplify the discussion of methods we will speak mainly of the death searches. This means that we may treat SEX, NAMES, DATES OF BIRTH, and GEOGRAPHICAL INFORMATION to do with the places of birth, work, residence, or death, as the primary personal identifiers for linkage. The principles and the practice, however, will be similar to those that apply to other kinds of linkage and to a wider diversity of identifiers.

For a manual search of a death file it is usual to array the records in alphabetical order under the surname followed by the given names or initials, much as in a telephone directory. The searcher, who is aware of the various ways in which certain of the surnames are spelled, may sometimes find it useful to look for a given individual in more than one place in the sequence. To avoid this, surnames can be phonetically coded and the files sequenced under the code followed by the full alphabetical information. This tactic is now routinely employed for the similar computer searches, often using a code known as 'NYSIIS' (New York State Intelligence Identification System). Only the records containing identical NYSIIS codes are then compared.

Where this approach fails and special measures are required to locate records that might have been missed due to spelling variations or changes of surname that alter the phonetic codes, an alternative sequence may sometimes be established for further searching. The one most commonly employed is in order of the first given name, followed by the year, month and day of birth, these being the next most reliable and discriminating identifiers available.

In this account it is assumed that the files initiating the searches, and those being searched, are similarly coded, formatted, and sequenced. This is to facilitate both the bringing together of pairs of records having the same surname codes, and the subsequent detailed comparisons of the other identifiers.

2

Probabilistic linkage: concepts and practice

'Linkage' in the present context is simply the bringing together of information from two records that are believed to relate to the same individual or family. Such records are said to be 'LINKED'. When one also calculates the likelihood of a correct linkage, and that the individual or family represented on the records is really the same, the process is said to be 'probabilistic'. There is nothing strange about the calculation, because a clerical searcher who carries out a similar operation manually, likewise forms an opinion on the degree of certainty that the records are correctly paired. The human logic may be intuitive and unconsciously applied, but it has the same basis as that which one wishes the machine to use.

The degree of certainty of a correct linkage obviously depends on the comparisons of the individual identifiers, and the outcomes from these comparisons. If all the identifiers agree and are unlikely to have done so by accident, the level of assurance will be high. Conversely, if they all disagree and are unlikely to have done so in truly linked pairs of records, there will be little doubt that the records in the pair are wrongly matched. For intermediate situations one must weigh the evidence, pro and con, to decide where the balance lies. Quantifying the process is not especially difficult.

The basic idea is very simple. If a NAME, or an INITIAL, or a MONTH OF BIRTH, or any other identifier, agrees or disagrees or is more or less similar or dissimilar in any way, one simply asks, 'How typical is that comparison outcome among LINKED pairs of records, as compared with UNLINKABLE pairs brought together at random?'

The reason why *agreements* will so often argue *for* linkage is that they are usually more typical of the LINKED pairs of records. And the reason why *disagreements* will usually argue *against* linkage is that they are, with a few exceptions, more typical of the UNLINKABLE pairs. The partial similarities or dissimilarities will sometimes argue in one direction and sometimes in the other, but this depends entirely on whether they are more typical of the LINKED pairs or the UNLINKABLE pairs.

These ratios are like betting odds. That is really all there is to the basic principle. There are some housekeeping details of course. The odds for the different identifier comparisons do need to be accumulated in some fashion for a given record pair, and one does need to know something about the LINKED and the UNLINKABLE pairs. But the concept is simple, precise, and intuitively obvious.

The logic is just what one would use when doing the job manually. Moreover, by doing it oneself one learns what one wants the machine to do.

3

Betting odds and frequency ratios

The basic principle used in probabilistic linkage may be represented by a simple FREQUENCY RATIO formula. The formula is just a restatement of the original question. It helps to demonstrate the diversity of situations in which the question may be asked, but the question itself remains unchanged throughout. Each FREQUENCY RATIO represents the 'betting ODDS' in favour of a correct match, associated with the particular comparison and its outcome.

For the comparison of any identifier on one member of a pair of records, with the same or a different identifier on the other record in the pair, and for any conceivable outcome or result from that comparison, defined in any way, the FREQUENCY RATIO is:

$$\frac{\text{FREQUENCY}}{\text{RATIO}} = \frac{\text{frequency of outcome } (x, y) \text{ among LINKED pairs}}{\text{frequency of outcome } (x, y) \text{ among UNLINKABLE pairs}}$$

where:

x indicates the identifier and its value on the record from the file initiating the search (record A);

y indicates the identifier and its value on the record from the file being searched (record B);

LINKED pairs may refer either to all linked pairs, or to a defined subset of these; and

UNLINKABLE pairs may refer either to all unlinkable pairs, or to a defined subset, provided the linked and the unlinkable sets (or subsets) are otherwise strictly comparable with each other.

All of the above is just a way of making the formula totally flexible and general. It does assume that one has established a file of LINKABLE pairs of records which, to the best of one's knowledge, are correctly matched. It also assumes that there is a comparison file of UNLINKABLE pairs that have been brought together at random. However, neither file has to be perfect in order to be useful. Small admixtures of false matches in the one, or of rejected true matches in the other, have only small effects on the accuracy of the FREQUENCY RATIO, or ODDS.

Let us consider some examples of the diversity of situations in which the basic question may be asked.

Examples — FIRST INITIALS
(1) AGREEMENT (any letter):

$$\frac{\text{FREQUENCY}}{\text{RATIO}} = \frac{\text{frequency of AGREEMENT among LINKED pairs}}{\text{frequency of AGREEMENT among UNLINKABLE pairs}} .$$

(2) DISAGREEMENT (any letter):

$$\frac{\text{FREQUENCY}}{\text{RATIO}} = \frac{\text{frequency of DISAGREEMENT among LINKED pairs}}{\text{frequency of DISAGREEMENT among UNLINKABLE pairs}} .$$

(3) AGREEMENT (letter 'Q'):

$$\frac{\text{FREQUENCY}}{\text{RATIO}} = \frac{\text{frequency of (Q,Q) among LINKED pairs}}{\text{frequency of (Q,Q) among UNLINKABLE pairs}} .$$

A number of options are left open in examples (1) to (3), regarding the way the LINKED and the UNLINKABLE pairs are chosen for the calculation:

(a) One may use all of the pairs in these two files.
(b) One may exclude from the calculation those pairs in which the identifier is missing from one or both of the records in the pair, on the grounds that no comparison is possible. This convenient simplification is widely employed, and any error it introduces is considered to be minor in most situations.
(c) In the case of the agreement of a specific letter ('Q'), it is simplest to base the calculation on just those pairs in which the search record (record A) has the specified field value for the first initial (i.e. 'Q'). Provided the search records that link are typical of the search file, this will not alter the FREQUENCY RATIO. What it does is bring both the numerator and the denominator closer to unity.

Examples — YEAR OF BIRTH
(4) SIMILARITY (difference = 1 year):

$$\text{FREQUENCY RATIO} = \frac{\text{frequency of (difference } = 1 \text{ yr.)} \\ \text{among LINKED pairs}}{\text{frequency of (difference } = 1 \text{ yr.)} \\ \text{among UNLINKABLE pairs}} \, .$$

(5) DISSIMILARITY (difference = 11 + years):

$$\text{FREQUENCY RATIO} = \frac{\text{frequency of (difference } = 11 + \\ \text{yrs.)} \\ \text{among LINKED pairs}}{\text{frequency of (difference } = 11 + \\ \text{yrs.)} \\ \text{among UNLINKABLE pairs}} \, .$$

Again, for examples (4) and (5) it will be simplest to base the calculation on just those LINKED and those UNLINKABLE pairs in which the identifier is represented on both records so that the comparison is possible. The same will be true for many of the examples that follow.

Examples — GIVEN NAMES:
(6) SIMILARITY (first three letters agree, none disagree — e.g. Sam vs. Samuel):

$$\text{FREQUENCY RATIO} = \frac{\text{frequency of (three agree, none disagree)} \\ \text{among LINKED pairs}}{\text{frequency of (three agree, none disagree)} \\ \text{among UNLINKABLE pairs}} \, .$$

(7) SIMILARITY + DISSIMILARITY (first three letters agree, fourth disagrees — e.g. Samuel vs. Sampson):

$$\text{FREQUENCY RATIO} = \frac{\text{frequency of (three agree, fourth disagrees)} \\ \text{among LINKED pairs}}{\text{frequency of (three agree, fourth disagrees)} \\ \text{among UNLINKABLE pairs}} \, .$$

Example — comparing *different but logically related identifiers*
(8) PLACE OF WORK vs. PLACE OF DEATH (Sudbury vs. Kenora):

$$\text{FREQUENCY RATIO} = \frac{\text{frequency of (Sudbury vs. Kenora)} \\ \text{among LINKED pairs}}{\text{frequency of (Sudbury vs. Kenora)} \\ \text{among UNLINKABLE pairs}} \, .$$

Because example (8) specifies particular identifier values, it is simplest to base the calculation on just those LINKED and UNLINKABLE pairs in which the record initiating the search (record A) carries the specified value (PLACE OF WORK = Sudbury). Value-specific FREQUENCY RATIOS are not altered by this practice, but the numerators and the denominators are both brought closer to unity and are simpler to handle.

In the above examples the FREQUENCY RATIO formula is completely flexible, in the sense that the basic question may be asked of any identifier comparison that seems likely to be profitable, and of any outcome from that comparison that is thought to be revealing.

How does one decide what identifiers to compare, and what outcomes from these comparisons should be recognized separately? The answer is simple. Just do some linkages manually and see what comparisons one makes oneself, and what outcomes from these comparisons provide useful clues in difficult cases. Concentrate on the linkages that require special thought, and do not overlook any of the logical steps that go on in one's own mind.

Collectively, the combined FREQUENCY RATIOS pertaining to a given record pair, i.e. their product, constitute the information on which the overall 'betting ODDS' in favour of (or against) a correct match are based.

4

Getting started

To calculate the FREQUENCY RATIOS one needs to know the frequencies of the various outcomes in a file of LINKED pairs of records, and in a corresponding file of UNLINKABLE pairs consisting of records brought together at random. Neither requirement presents any great difficulty.

If one is starting from scratch, the LINKED pairs are best obtained by manually searching and matching, using appropriately sequenced files. These linkages do not have to be perfect to be useful, and the numbers need not be large. Any such linked set will normally contain a small admixture of record pairs that have been wrongly matched, and it will usually fail to include some of the potential correct matches that ought to be included. However, the resulting inaccuracies will only be important if they substantially alter the calculated frequencies of discrepancies and partial discrepancies in that file. One could make do initially with just a few hundred LINKED pairs, but a thousand would enable the percentage rates for disagreement and partial disagreement to be calculated to one decimal point. This file will be enlarged and improved later anyway as the automated linkage progresses and as the doubtful links are scrutinized.

Where a linkage operation has already been carried out earlier using a different file to initiate the searches, the outcome frequencies from the previous operation are sometimes employed initially in designing the new linkage procedure. This may be all right, but only if the two search files are of similar quality (e.g. as when the identifiers are wrongly reported with similar frequencies in the two of them), and provided also that the file being searched is the same (e.g. the same death file). The reasoning applies whether discrepancies of the identifiers are due to error or to legitimate changes with time.

There is less immediate need for a file of UNLINKABLE pairs of records, provided the comparison procedures are kept simple. The reason is that one can often calculate easily what the outcome frequencies would be in such a file. This is true, for example, of the likelihood of chance agreements of MONTH OF BIRTH, because there are only 12 of them and these tend to be about equally represented in both the search file (file A) and the file being searched (file B). It is true also of NAME agreements and disagreements, as long as one is not dealing with the partial agreements. In principle, of course, one may predict theoretically the frequency of almost any outcome in a file of randomly matched pairs. In practice, however, some of the calculations are too tedious for routine use, while others are confusing and prone to error even in skilled hands. At some point in this spectrum of complexity it is simpler to create and use a real file of UNLINKABLE pairs.

To get started with probabilistic linkage, it is best to keep the comparison procedures simple. Then only the file of LINKED pairs is needed initially.

5

A simplified procedure: using 'global' discriminating powers

To illustrate how the probabilistic linkage works it is best to start with a simple example. For this purpose we will recognize only the full AGREEMENT and the DISAGREEMENT outcomes from the comparisons of the various identifiers, and will calculate only the FREQUENCY RATIOS that are non-specific for the 'value' of an identifier when it does agree. As a further simplification we will assume in the example that the identifiers selected for comparison are always present on the records of both the search file (file A) and the file being searched (file B). Likely magnitudes of the FREQUENCY RATIOS are shown in Table 5.1.

The FREQUENCY RATIOS in Table 5.1 show the extent to which each identifier influences the overall 'betting ODDS', depending on whether it *agrees* or *disagrees*. However, these ODDS do not take into account whether the particular SURNAME, when it agrees, is a rare or a common name. The same is true of the FIRST NAME and MIDDLE INITIAL, and of the PROVINCE or FOREIGN COUNTRY OF BIRTH.

Table 5.1 Global frequency ratios for agreements and disagreements of identifiers on matched pairs of records

Identifiers compared	Comparison outcomes	Percentage frequencies		Global frequency ratios (links/non-links)
		Links	Non-links	
SURNAME	Agree	96.5	0.1	965/1
	Disagree	3.5	99.9	1/29
FIRST NAME	Agree	79.0	0.9	88/1
	Disagree	21.0	99.1	1/5
MIDDLE INITIAL	Agree	88.8	7.5	12/1
	Disagree	11.2	92.5	1/8

Table 5.1—*Continued*

Identifiers compared	Comparison outcomes	Percentage frequencies		Global frequency ratios (links/non-links)
		Links	Non-links	
YEAR OF BIRTH	Agree	77.3	1.1	70/1
	Disagree	22.7	98.9	1/4
MONTH OF BIRTH	Agree	93.3	8.3	11/1
	Disagree	6.7	91.7	1/14
DAY OF BIRTH	Agree	85.1	3.3	26/1
	Disagree	14.9	96.7	1/6
PROVINCE/COUNTRY OF BIRTH	Agree	98.1	11.7	8/1
	Disagree	1.9	88.3	1/46

6

A more efficient procedure: using 'specific' discriminating powers

In the example in Chapter 5, the FREQUENCY RATIOS took no account of the discriminating power of the particular NAME, INITIAL, or PLACE OF BIRTH. Thus such SURNAMES as Brown, Aube, or Skuda would all be represented by identical FREQUENCY RATIOS when they agreed, as would the given names John, Axel, or Ulder, the initials B, Z, or Q, and the PLACES OF BIRTH Ontario, Prince Edward Island, or New Zealand. These FREQUENCY RATIOS are said to be 'global'.

In actual practice, such global FREQUENCY RATIOS are routinely converted to their 'value-specific' counterparts wherever this would result in better use being made of the discriminating power of the identifiers. The conversion is not difficult for the full agreements. A search record containing the first given name John will encounter other records with the same name, purely by accident, with a frequency equal to that in the file it is searching. So one can predict this frequency without actually creating a file of UNLINKABLE pairs. Examples of these frequencies are given in Table 6.1.

It has been the custom to store in look-up tables the frequencies of 'specific' values for such identifiers, as they appear in the file being searched (e.g. a death file). The practice is particularly appropriate where the values of possible interest are too numerous to be conveniently incorporated directly into the instructions to the computer.

Table 6.1 Frequencies of 'specific' values of identifiers in the file being searched, e.g. a death file (These are equal to the *'Specific' frequencies of full agreements among unlinkable pairs* where the search record carries the specified 'value' of the identifier. The final column in the Table could, in fact, carry that heading.)

Kind of identifier	'Value' of that identifier on the search record	'Specific' frequency in the file being searched (%)
SURNAME	Brown	0.39
	Aube	0.014
	Skuda	0.00004
FIRST NAME (male)	John	5.30
	Axel	0.020
	Ulder	0.0045
INITIAL (male)	J	15.55
	Z	0.10
	Q	0.023
PLACE OF BIRTH	Ontario	19.7
	Prince Edward Island	1.03
	New Zealand	0.020

7

Recognizing degrees of similarity

Often an identifier may fail to agree precisely on a pair of records but be obviously similar nevertheless. Examples include slightly discrepant date of birth components, names that are sometimes truncated or differ in a few final letters, and geographical locations that are in proximity but are not quite the same. Dissimilarities are of course a part of the spectrum so that even disagreements are rarely absolute and can likewise differ in degree. The judgement of a human searcher may be strongly influenced by his or her perception of these partial similarities and dissimilarities. The machine would make poor use of the discriminating powers contained in the identifiers if it could not do as the human does in this matter. Some examples arising out of a death search will illustrate the point (see Table 7.1).

Discriminating power would be obviously wasted if one were to lump in the intermediate levels of PARTIAL AGREEMENT with either the FULL AGREEMENTS or the more extreme DISAGREEMENTS. Indeed, it would even be profitable to further subdivide the levels of agreement and disagreement (or of similarity and dissimilarity, or of logical relationship of any kind), up to the point at which the adjacent levels of outcome created in this way cease to differ substantially (e.g. by more than factor 2) in the FREQUENCY RATIOS they yield.

Table 7.1 Frequencies ratios for different levels of agreement of identifiers (based on work records compared with death records)

Identifiers compared	Comparison outcomes	Percentage frequencies		Frequency ratios (links/ non-links)
		Links	Non-links	
YEAR OF BIRTH				
	Full agreement	77.3	1.1	72/1
	Difference = 1 yr.	15.1	2.2	7/1
	Difference = 2+ yrs.	7.6	96.7	1/13
GIVEN NAME (initial already agrees)				
	Full agreement	83.1	14.0	6/1
	First four characters agree	5.8	1.6	4/1
	Disagreement in first four characters	11.1	84.4	1/8
PLACE OF WORK vs. PLACE OF DEATH (Ontario miners)				
	Same Ontario mining area	54.3	0.5	106/1
	Different Ontario mining areas	10.6	1.8	6/1
	Death in non-mining area	35.1	97.7	1/3

8

Conditional comparisons versus concatenated identifiers

Identifiers that are logically related may appear on the records as separate identifiers, and sometimes as just a single identifier. Examples include PROVINCE plus LOCALITY (of residence or work or death), and FIRST INITIAL plus remainder of the FIRST GIVEN NAME. There are two ways of dealing with these:

1. The two parts may be compared separately, with the second comparison being *conditional* upon the outcome from the first.
2. The two parts may be combined or *concatenated*, with recognition of a number of possible levels of outcome from the comparison.

One should choose whichever option offers the most revealing outcomes, the simplest logic, or the greatest convenience, in that order of importance. With either choice, care is required to avoid pitfalls in calculating the FREQUENCY RATIOS.

If one compares the PROVINCE first, and then the LOCALITY within the province, the second of the two comparisons will be *conditional* upon an AGREEMENT outcome from the first comparison. There is little point in comparing the LOCALITY where the PROVINCE is already known to disagree (unless PROVINCE is an unreliable field). The same reasoning holds if one decides to compare the FIRST INITIAL separately, and follow with a further comparison of the remainder of the FIRST GIVEN NAME. With the two-comparison procedure special care must be taken in calculating the FREQUENCY RATIOS: where the PROVINCE agrees, the frequency with which the LOCALITY also agrees must be calculated *within* that PROVINCE (as distinct from the country as a whole). Where the FIRST INITIAL agrees the frequency with which the remainder of the FIRST GIVEN NAME also agrees must be calculated *within* that INITIAL (as distinct from all initials); this is done routinely now and works well, but a beginner might choose otherwise to start with.

If one decides instead to use a single-comparison procedure in

Table 8.1 Procedures using conditional comparisons versus concatenated identifiers

Identifiers compared	Comparison outcomes	Percentage frequencies		Frequency ratios (links/ non-links)
		Links	Non-links	
Procedures employing a conditional comparison				
PROVINCE				
	Agree	91.6	35.1	3/1
	Disagree	8.4	64.9	1/8
LOCALITY				
(compared only if PROVINCE agrees)				
	Agree (within that province)	59.3	1.4	42/1
	Disagree	40.7	98.6	1/2
FIRST INITIAL				
	Agree	94.0	6.9	14/1
	Disagree	6.0	93.1	1/16
Remainder of GIVEN NAME				
(compared only if INITIAL agrees)				
	Agree (within that unit)	84.0	12.4	7/1
	Disagree	16.0	87.6	1/5
Procedures employing concatenated identifiers				
PROVINCE and LOCALITY				
	Both agree	54.3	0.5	106/1
	Province agrees, locality disagrees	37.3	34.6	1/1
	Province disagrees	8.4	64.9	1/8
INITIAL and remainder of				
FIRST GIVEN NAME				
	Both agree	79.0	0.9	88/1
	Initial agrees, remainder disagrees	15.0	6.0	3/1
	Initial disagrees	6.0	93.1	1/16

which the components of the identifier are *concatenated*, a number of levels of outcome will have to be recognized separately. The advantage of this tactic is that the logic is simpler and the FREQUENCY RATIOS are less confusing to calculate; they are therefore less likely to be wrong.

The single-comparison procedure using concatenated identifiers, by its nature, provides a simple check which is capable of revealing the most likely errors of logic; in other words, if the frequencies do not add up to 100 per cent, something is wrong. This may seem obvious for the outcome frequencies among LINKED pairs. It is less so, however, for the UNLINKABLE pairs, particularly where there is no such actual file and the frequencies are being calculated or estimated instead of measured. For procedures employing conditional comparisons such a test would be more complicated and less obvious, especially where there is a series of conditional comparisons.

The two procedures are compared in Table 8.1, and the result is the same for both. FREQUENCY RATIOS for the separate AGREEMENTS in a two-comparison approach must, of course, be multiplied with each other before they can be compared with those for the double AGREEMENTS in the single-comparison approach. (The RATIOS in Table 8.1 are rounded, but any discrepancy due to this will disappear when the calculation is carried to an adequate number of places.) Only if one goes beyond the rules applied above will the answers differ.

9

Converting 'global' odds to 'specific' odds

It is customary to do a preliminary linkage based solely on *global* FREQUENCY RATIOS or *global* ODDS such as those shown in Table 5.1, and then to convert these to their *value-specific* counterparts wherever that will ensure better use of the available discriminating power. The first of the two steps greatly reduces the number of candidate pairs for linkage, and leaves only a much smaller number requiring the conversion. This Chapter deals with the manner in which the conversion may be carried out.

(For reasons of convenience the outcome frequencies among LINKED and UNLINKABLE pairs of records, and the ratios of the two frequencies, are often expressed as logarithms. Where this is done the logarithms are called 'weights'. The global FREQUENCY RATIO or global ODDS for a given comparison outcome then becomes a net global weight. The use of the logarithms and of the term 'weight' does not alter the rationale, which is more readily visualized without them.)

Conversion of the global FREQUENCY RATIOS or global ODDS to their value-specific counterparts is a crucial step in the overall linkage operation. The concept is simple enough. Moreover, a satisfactory practice exists that is applicable equally to the full agreements and to the partial agreements, but which has so far not come into general use. The chief purpose of the present Chapter is to describe this generally applicable procedure. In particular, any such method must work well with the partial agreements of SURNAMES, INITIALS, and GIVEN NAMES, and must be unlikely to be wrongly applied in routine practice.

9.1. Specific odds for full agreements

Conceptually, the conversion from a *global* FREQUENCY RATIO (or *global* ODDS) to a *value-specific* FREQUENCY RATIO (or *specific* ODDS) is just a matter of specifying how the basic formula is to be used. In practice, however, both the numerator and the denominator of the value-specific version of that formula are usually estimated, as distinct from being actually observed or measured. This will be clearer if we look for a moment at the two versions of the formula, given below:

(1) the global FREQUENCY RATIO

$$= \frac{\text{frequency of AGREEMENT in LINKED pairs (record A has } any \text{ value)}}{\text{frequency of AGREEMENT in UNLINKABLE pairs (record A has } any \text{ value)}}$$

(2) the value-specific FREQUENCY RATIO

$$= \frac{\text{frequency of AGREEMENT in LINKED pairs (record A has } specified \text{ value)}}{\text{frequency of AGREEMENT in UNLINKABLE pairs (record A has } specified \text{ value)}}$$

where record A of a matched pair is the one from the file that initiated the searches.

When the conversion is carried out from a global FREQUENCY RATIO to a specific FREQUENCY RATIO, the process is simplified by *estimating* both components of the latter RATIO, rather than actually measuring them. Thus:

1. For DISAGREEMENTS, the FREQUENCY RATIOS are not actually converted from the 'global' to the 'value specific'. Instead, the *assumption* is made that the particular value of the identifier on record A does not greatly influence the chance of a DISAGREEMENT. In other words, the global ODDS for a given disagreement are unchanged and now serve as an *estimate* of what the true specific ODDS would have been had they been measured.

2. For FULL AGREEMENTS, the NUMERATORS of the FREQUENCY RATIOS are likewise not actually converted from the 'global' to the 'value specific'. It is *assumed* instead that, in the linked pairs, the particular value of the identifier on record A does not greatly influence the chance of an AGREEMENT. In other words, the global NUMERATOR for a given AGREEMENT is unchanged and now serves as an *estimate* of what the true value-specific NUMERATOR would have been had it been measured.

3. For FULL AGREEMENTS, the DENOMINATORS of the FREQUENCY

RATIOS are also not actually converted from the 'global' to the 'value specific'. It is *inferred* instead that the frequency, in the unlinkable pairs, of a chance AGREEMENT of the particular value of the identifier on record A will be identical to the frequency of that 'specific' value in the file being searched (file B). In other words, the specific FREQUENCY of the value in file B serves as an *estimate* of what the true value-specific DENOMINATOR would have been had it been measured.

The assumptions contained in 1. and 2. above may be viewed as tolerable approximations to the truth, whereas the inference in 3. is probably precisely correct. The best reason for following this route is that, for very rare values of an identifier, even large files of LINKED and UNLINKABLE pairs may sometimes be too small to provide adequate data of the strictly applicable kinds. Some of the estimates might therefore be better than the actual measurements one is likely to get, as well as being easier to obtain.

When dealing solely with FULL AGREEMENTS and with DISAGREEMENTS, the above practices are simple despite the apparent deviousness. The only thing that gets changed in the conversion process is the denominator of the FREQUENCY RATIO formula for the AGREEMENTS. For this denominator, one merely substitutes the value-specific frequency from the file being searched.

It is with the PARTIAL AGREEMENTS that such a simple approach cannot be used. It leads to biases, and these may sometimes be large enough to be grossly misleading.

9.2. Specific odds for partial agreements

For PARTIAL AGREEMENTS such as those of the SURNAMES and GIVEN NAMES, the above procedure would be incorrect and often considerably in error. In the conversion of a global FREQUENCY RATIO to its value-specific counterpart, the frequency of the particular value in the file being searched cannot be used as an *estimate* of what the value-specific DENOMINATOR would have been. Our task, therefore, is to explain why this is so, and to describe a correct method for making the conversion where the agreement is only partial.

The added complication with the PARTIAL AGREEMENTS arises because these are defined not just by the part of the identifier that agrees, but also by the part that fails to agree (i.e. disagrees, or is missing on one of the records). The non-agreement part of the definition creates a subset out of the larger body of record pairs that would have been defined by the agreement part alone. The percentage frequency of the particular outcome level, in both the LINKED and the UNLINKED pairs, is therefore necessarily reduced because of the disagreement part of its definition. The usual *estimate* for the value-specific DENOMINATOR now becomes inappropriate; it is no longer comparable with the NUMERATOR because it has not been reduced in magnitude in the same way as the numerator.

No problem would arise if one could stick strictly to the formula in which the numerator and the denominator of the FREQUENCY RATIO both continue to be defined in precisely the same way as each other, both before and after conversion. The two versions of the basic formula may be compared thus

1. The *global* FREQUENCY RATIO for PARTIAL AGREEMENTS

$$= \frac{\text{frequency of (AGREEMENT + DISAGREEMENT)}}{\text{frequency of (AGREEMENT + DISAGREEMENT)}}_{\text{in UNLINKABLE pairs (record A has }any\text{ value)}} .$$

2. The *value-specific* FREQUENCY RATIO for PARTIAL AGREEMENTS

$$= \frac{\text{frequency of (AGREEMENT + DISAGREEMENT) in}}{\text{frequency of (AGREEMENT + DISAGREEMENT) in}}_{\text{UNLINKABLE pairs (record A has }specific\text{ value)}} .$$

There is no problem with the 'global' version of this formula because both the numerator and the denominator can be obtained from real files of LINKED and UNLINKABLE pairs. There is also no particular problem with the numerator of the 'specific' version of the formula, because as seen earlier the global NUMERATOR is considered good enough to serve as a substitute for the value-specific NUMERATOR.

It is the DENOMINATOR that creates the complication. This time it would be improper to simply substitute as a DENOMINATOR the frequency of the agreement portion of the identifier as found in the file being searched. That frequency would overestimate the DENOMINATOR because the latter ought correctly to relate only to a subset of the larger number of pairs in which the agreement occurs with *and* without the disagreement. The problem is that of avoiding the resulting mismatch between NUMERATOR and

DENOMINATOR, which would bias the RATIO downwards, sometimes substantially so.

Stated another way, a global DENOMINATOR (or a global numerator) represents the full definition of the comparison outcome, including the agreement part *and* the non-agreement part. It can do this because it is based on *pairs* of records that are compared with each other, as distinct from *unpaired* records. One cannot replace a global frequency with any frequency ('general' or 'specific') drawn from the file being searched, because that file is made up of single, *unpaired* records. The global frequencies and frequency ratios are of a different kind. True, in the special case of the full agreements the numerical distinction may disappear, but the conceptual distinction remains.

A theoretical solution that is *not* reommended here is to calculate the DENOMINATOR using detailed data drawn from both the search file (file A) and the file being searched (file B). For the inexperienced, the calculation is apt to be difficult and confusing, and it is almost certain to be error prone. As well, such calculations can be exceedingly time consuming for anyone, no matter how skilled. So the theoretical solution is unlikely to be sufficiently convenient and reliable to come into routine use, especially where it may have to be adapted from time to time to accommodate changes of the comparison rules or the compositions of the names. (The theoretical approach is considered at greater length in the Appendices.)

Rather than describe such calculations in this Chapter, we consider instead a possible simpler approach which is equally precise. This involves practically no calculation, but does require a real file of UNLINKABLE pairs of records.

9.3. A simple procedure that will work with both full and partial agreements

What is proposed is a simplified but correct procedure whereby the *global* FREQUENCY RATIOS for both the PARTIAL AGREEMENTS and the FULL AGREEMENTS may be converted to become *value specific*. The use of a real life of UNLINKABLE pairs of records enables us to bypass the theoretical calculations.

This simplified procedure does not discard any part of the global FREQUENCY RATIO. Instead, the global RATIO is converted to its value-specific counterpart by an adjustment upwards or downwards, depending on whether the agreement portion of the specific identifier is rare or common in comparison with the 'average' or 'general' frequency for that portion of the identifier. The extent and direction of this adjustment are determined by comparing the value-specific frequency in the file being searched, with the general frequency as derived from the same file. (The general frequency has been commonly used as an estimate of the global agreement frequency in unlinkable pairs of records, but it has served no valid purpose in the past with respect to the partial agreement outcomes.)

The *general* frequency for an identifier such as a surname or a given name, or for any truncated form of these, may be viewed as a weighted mean of all the specific frequencies in the file being searched (file B). The weighting for each value is by how often that value would be involved in a fortuitous agreement among randomly matched pairs when the file is searched (i.e. by the records from file A). Strictly speaking, the general frequency is a summation of the products of the specific frequencies for corresponding values of all identifiers in the two files. It is usual, however, to assume that the specific frequencies are the same in file A and file B. The general frequency then becomes the sum of the squares of all the specific frequencies in the file being searched (file B).

Thus, for any identifier (e.g. the surname or the first name), or any portion of that identifier (e.g. truncated versions of these), the formula normally used is:

General frequency = sum of (frequency of value '*x*')^2 summed over all values of '*x*'.

If we divide this general frequency by the value-specific frequency for a particular name, the result will be greater than unity where the name is rare and carries high discriminating power. Conversely, if the name is common and carries little discriminating POWER the result will be less than unity. We may call this an ADJUSTMENT FACTOR or, if we wish to distinguish it from other possible adjustment factors, a 'specific' ADJUSTMENT. When the global FREQUENCY RATIO is multiplied by the adjustment factor, the ratio is 'adjusted' upwards or downwards to become a value-specific

FREQUENCY RATIO. Such an adjustment may be applied to the agreement portion of any surname or given name that is being compared, whether there is FULL AGREEMENT or just PARTIAL AGREEMENT.

A few examples will illustrate how the adjustment works. Let us consider the following comparisons of first given names:

(1) SAMUEL–SAMUEL (full agreement);
(2) SAMPSON–SAMPSON (full agreement);
(3) *SAM–SAMU*EL (partial agreement; 3 agree + missing characters);
(4) *SAM*PSON–*SAM*UEL (partial agreement; 3 agree + disagreement).

The relevant *general* frequencies, derived from a file of death records, are:

(1), (2) male given names, all lengths up to 7 characters   = 1·15 per cent.
(3), (4) male given names, truncated at 3 characters   = 1·47 per cent.

The relevant *specific* frequencies, from the same source, are:

(1)   SAMUEL   = 18 927/3 534 476 = 0.54   per cent.
(2)   SAMPSON =   82/3 534 476 = 0.0023 per cent.
(3), (4) SAM   = 21 617/3 534 476 = 0.61   per cent.

The relevant *global* FREQUENCY RATIOS for male given names are shown in the Table:

Comparison outcomes (male given names)	Percentage frequencies		Global frequency ratios (links/non-links)
	Links	Non-links	
FULL AGREEMENT (any length up to 7 Characters)	78.11	0.97	78/1
PARTIAL AGREEMENT (3 agree + missing Characters)	0.38	0.01	38/1
PARTIAL AGREEMENT (3 agree + disagree)	3.10	0.28	11/1

We may now 'adjust' the global FREQUENCY RATIOS so they become value specific, as in the following Table:

Characters of the given name	Name pairs under comparison			
	SAMUEL SAMUEL	SAMPSON SAMPSON	*SAM SAMUEL*	*SAMPSON SAMUEL*
Global frequency ratio (full *or* partial agreement)	78/1	78/1	38/1	11/1
General frequency (agreement portion of the name) (%)	1.15	1.15	1.47	1.47
Specific frequency (%)	0.54	0.0023	0.61	0.61
Adjustment factor (general/specific)	2.1	500.0	2.4	2.4
Value-specific frequency ratio (= global × adjustment)	164/1	39000/1	91/1	26/1

In these examples, all the ADJUSTMENT FACTORS happen to be greater than unity, and the FREQUENCY RATIOS are increased when converted to their value-specific form. For the more common given names, however, the reverse would be the case. For example, for the name JOHN (specific frequency 187 000/3 534 476 = 5.29%, in a Canadian file of male deaths) the ADJUSTMENT FACTOR would be 1.15/5.29 = 0.22, and the FREQUENCY RATIO would be decreased when it became value specific. If some value of the name happened to have a precisely 'average' frequency, there would have been no change at all when the conversion takes place. This is all as it should be.

The virtues of this approach are that it avoids complicated calculations, it is equally applicable to both the FULL AGREEMENTS and the PARTIAL AGREEMENTS, and it is flexible enough to accommodate readily any changes in the comparison rules. The mechanics are simple; instead of the look-up tables containing the specific frequencies they would contain the specific ADJUSTMENT FACTORS, i.e. the general frequency divided by the specific frequencies. Separate look-up tables would, of course, be prepared for the different degrees of truncation.

In this way one is able to bypass the theory by using a real file of UNLINKABLE pairs. However, the empirical and the theoretical approaches should give identical answers.

10

Accumulating the odds

What is needed from the comparisons of the various identifiers on a given record pair is some sort of overall indication of the degree of assurance of a correct match, which we might call the 'combined ODDS' or 'OVERALL ODDS'. This is provided by multiplying all of the FREQUENCY RATIOS for the pair, with each other. It is customary to accomplish the multiplication by first converting each of the FREQUENCY RATIOS into its logarithm, called a 'WEIGHT', and then adding the WEIGHTS to produce a 'TOTAL WEIGHT'. The process assumes that the various agreements and disagreements are independent of each other. At this stage, the resulting OVERALL ODDS or TOTAL WEIGHT is only a relative measure of the assurance of a correct link, not an absolute measure. It serves chiefly to rank the matched pairs in order of this assurance.

The assumption that the agreements and disagreements of the different identifiers are independent of each other may not be strictly correct. However, some simple precautions will ensure that the bias from this source is small. For example, if a matched pair of documents has in common the province or foreign country of birth, not only of the individual but also of the two parents, one should be aware that these are highly likely to be correlated with each other. Where the three individuals all had the same place of birth it would obviously be improper to attach any special significance to a resulting triple agreement. Alternatively, if the three individuals each had a different place of birth, and the two records were in agreement on the matter, then use could legitimately be made of the triple agreement. Also, disagreements may sometimes be correlated and then should not be taken too seriously as arguing collectively against a correct match; multiple wrong guesses on the part of an informant are probably a common source of such correlations. An awareness of this possibility is useful when manually checking a group of borderline linkages. Formal procedures have been devised for dealing quantitatively with such correlations but tend to be laborious and largely unrewarding. Common sense usually tells one when to avoid the 'double weighting' of information that is essentially the same.

Since much of the literature on record linkage speaks of WEIGHTS instead of FREQUENCY RATIOS, the reader should know that the two represent essentially the same thing. Logarithms to the base 2 are often employed as the WEIGHTS, because they are readily visualized and can be calculated on one's fingers. The logarithm of the numerator is always negative and is sometimes called a 'TRANSMISSION WEIGHT'. That of the denominator is always positive; in the case of a FULL AGREEMENT, the denominator has been termed a 'FREQUENCY WEIGHT'. In view of these usages, the logarithm of the FREQUENCY RATIO itself has been referred to as a 'NET WEIGHT', i.e. the sum of a positive and a negative weight. Although the transmission and the frequency components are also termed 'WEIGHTS', they are really just components of a ratio; like any numerator and denominator they lose much of their meaning when separated from each other. Care is required to preserve this subtle distinction when dealing with WEIGHTS.

11

Doing without a file of unlinkable pairs

In the course of a linkable operation, a file of LINKED pairs of records is created automatically as a product. This should be used to measure directly, and update, the NUMERATORS of the global FREQUENCY RATIOS. The discussion up to this point has assumed that a corresponding file of randomly matched UNLINKABLE pairs would be created to provide similarly direct information about the global DENOMINATORS. Until recently, however, few files of the latter kind have actually been created. The reason was that, for many of the comparisons, the likely outcome frequencies in such a file could be calculated or estimated. But the problem of the others remained. It would be useful to indicate here, those of the comparison procedures for which such calculations are simple and those for which they are not.

For the comparisons of dates of birth the calculations are not too difficult. As there are only 12 months in a year and the births are fairly uniformly distributed among them, it is easy to predict for the month of birth the random frequencies of FULL AGREEMENT, different levels of PARTIAL AGREEMENT, and the more extreme DISAGREEMENTS. The same is true for the day of birth. The year of birth is a different matter because these are rarely uniformly distributed, and the two files involved in the linkages (e.g. a work file versus a death file) will usually differ from each other with respect to the distribution. The calculation is tedious rather than difficult, but this is enough to make people disinclined to repeat it each time a new linkage job occurs. Where an actual file of UNLINKABLE pairs is created, all of these outcome frequencies become as readily obtainable for DENOMINATORS as they are for NUMERATORS.

It is the PARTIAL AGREEMENT outcomes for the comparisons of names that present the greatest problem where no real file of UNLINKABLE pairs of records exists. The calculations are possible; but they are difficult, time consuming, and error prone. Moreover, the data on which they must be based are best extracted from both of the files being linked, and are almost certain to change with the job. Thus, for a routine operation with a diverse succession of jobs it is unlikely that the calculations will be repeated each time. Those carrying out the linkages will undoubtedly find it easiest to assume that every job is exactly like the previous one, and thereby avoid having to repeat the calculations over again, in time for each new job.

Experience so far with real files of UNLINKABLE pairs has shown that these not only circumvent the major problem of handling the name comparisons efficiently, but simplify many others as well. Their uses are considered further as we proceed.

Part II

Exploiting more of the discriminating power

12

Deciding what comparison outcomes
to recognize

The relatively simple comparison procedures described up to this point are adequate for many linkage operations. But they do not fully exploit the discriminating power inherent in the identifiers. One learns this when examining visually the more ambiguous borderline links. There will be clues that are obvious to the perceptive human but not to the machine when working to the rules discussed so far.

Whether one wishes to go to greater lengths to tap more fully the available discriminating power will depend on the nature of the job and one's own inclinations when designing the procedures. However, where the numbers of false-positive links and missed linkages are important, and where the time spent doing manual resolutions is to be kept to a minimum, some further sophistication in the comparison procedures could be well worth the effort. After all, once a more appropriately precise comparison procedure has been developed and tested, this may be used repeatedly often with only minor modification or none at all.

There are a few general guidelines for those who want to develop better comparison procedures. The first is to spend considerable time resolving the difficult bordeline links manually, to see how one's own mind works when seeking clues that will help to reduce the uncertainty. Does one make unconventional comparisons? And, does one recognize as separate outcomes, shades of similarity or dissimilarity that a machine might miss if not told to look for them? The second rule is to do initially a much finer breakdown of the outcome levels than appears strictly necessary. One can always later recombine those adjacent levels of outcome that yield essentially similar FREQUENCY RATIOS (e.g. ratios that are within a factor 2 of each other). Conversely, wherever there are substantial differences in the FREQUENCY RATIOS, the outcome levels that yield these should *not* be pooled but should continue to be recognized separately.

In the chapters of Part II we consider each of the major identifiers, to see how much general guidelines for improving the comparison procedures may best be applied.

13

What to do with missing identifiers

By far the simplest thing to do when an identififer is missing from one or both of a pair of records is to regard the comparison as indicating nothing. The FREQUENCY RATIO, if one uses it at all, is taken to be unity. However, the underlying assumption that blank fields are essentially neutral is probably only approximately true in many instances, and in just a few cases it is substantially wrong.

A special situation in which the missing identifiers are far from neutral arises when linking the records of infant deaths back to the appropriate birth records. A missing name on the death record usually indicates that the child died before it was given a name, in which case the birth record will presumably likewise lack the name. (It has not been customary to speak of 'agreement' and 'disagreement' with respect to the presence or absence of an identifier, so we will use the terms 'concordance' and discordance' instead.) CONCORDANCES of the above kind are apt to argue strongly in favour of a correct linkage, and DISCORDANCE may argue in the opposite direction. When doing this sort of linkage it would therefore be prudent to calculate the relevant FREQUENCY RATIOS, rather as if the blank space were a name of sorts.

There is a more common situation in which a missing identifier carries positive discriminating power when it is concordant. This has to do with the middle name or initial. Some people do not have a middle name, or they may habitually fail to use it. For the linked pairs of records pertaining to such individuals, the absences will tend to be concordant. The associated FREQUENCY RATIOS are sometimes substantial for such concordances, and also for the corresponding discordances although in the opposite direction. An example is given in Chapter 15.

The short answer to the question 'What does one do with missing identifiers?' is: when in doubt, calculate the FREQUENCY RATIOS for concordances and for discordances, to see whether there is enough discriminating power there to justify retaining such a refinement.

14

Comparing surnames

The usual practice when comparing SURNAMES is to phonetically code the SURNAME, and to compare both the coded version and the full alphabetical name. A number of levels of agreement, partial agreement, and more extreme disagreement may be recognized separately in the outcomes from this comparison. Where the blocking of the files is based on the surname phonetic code, this code will not be allowed to disagree. However, a disagreement outcome for the phonetic code will be possible where the linkage is carried out under some alternative sequence, as when the probabilistic procedures are applied to check the validity of prior linkages under a numerical identifier like the Canadian Social Insurance Number (SIN) or the American Social Security Number (SSN).

The levels of partial agreement of the alphabetical surname are best decided upon after looking at a list of surname pairs that have failed to agree precisely in records known to be correctly linked. One might then base the levels of partial agreement on the numbers of characters that agree, when the phonetic code has already agreed. An example of how the FREQUENCY RATIOS would look in such a scheme is given in Table 14.1. The phonetic code used in this com-

Table 14.1 Global frequency ratios for different levels of agreement of surnames

Comparison outcomes (surname phonetic code plus 7 alphabetical characters compared)	Percentage frequencies		Global frequency ratios (links/non-links)
	Links	Non-links	
FULL AGREEMENT (any length up to 7)	96.5	0.042	1856/1
Code + first 4 characters agree	1.6	0.004	400/1
Code only agrees	1.9	0.034	56/1
Code disagrees	(0.0)	99.920	(not applicable)

parison is that of the New York State Intelligence Information System (NYSIIS). Other comparisons, done after a prior linkage using the Social Insurance Number (SIN), have shown that the NYSIIS code may disagree among correctly linked pairs with a frequency of about 2 per cent.

15

Comparing and cross-comparing initials

Comparison of the INITIALS is a particularly important part of the overall comparison procedures. Much depends on how it is done, and it is worth spending time to ensure that such comparison serves a number of purposes. There are special uses of the initials that would be lost if these identifiers were treated merely as shortened versions of the GIVEN NAMES.

Three major considerations determine how the comparisons may be best carried out:

1. *Absences* of the MIDDLE NAME or INITIAL are not without discriminating power, the magnitude of which is measured most simply in a comparison procedure for the INITIALS alone.
2. The discriminating powers of the two INITIALS are likely to be *correlated* with each other, and the possible bias from this source is not readily predicted. It may be avoided entirely, however, by concatenating the two INITIALS and treating them together in a single comparison procedure with multiple levels of outcome.
3. Because people may reverse the order of their GIVEN NAMES, *cross-comparisons* of the names are sometimes required. Prior comparison of the INITIALS, including cross-comparison where there is no straight agreement, is the simplest way to determine where a cross-comparison of the remainders of the given names is likely to be worth while.

Table 15.1 Global frequency ratios for concordance and for discordance with respect to missing middle initials

Comparison outcomes (middle initials present or absent)	Percentage frequencies		Global frequency ratios (links/non-links)
	Links	Non-links	
Present on both members of the pair	61.8	42.5	1.5/1
Missing on one, present on the other	6.8	45.4	1/6.7
Missing on both	31.4	12.1	2.6/1

Moreover, some simplification of the comparison procedure for the full given names results from separating out the numerous instances in which only the initial is present to be compared.

The discriminating power of a missing MIDDLE INITIAL, when concordant and when discordant, may be measured as shown in Table 15.1. The discriminating power revealed in the Table is considerable. There is an approximate 17-fold difference in the FREQUENCY RATIOS for 'missing on both' as compared with 'missing on one'. This amount of potential added assurance should not be lightly ignored.

A detailed comparison scheme for the concatenated initials that will serve all of the above purposes is shown in Table 15.2. The conversions of these 'global' FREQUENCY RATIOS into their 'value-specific' counterparts would be carried out as described in Chapter 9. Where there are two agreements or cross-agreements in a particular outcome, two ADJUSTMENT FACTORS are applied, one for

Table 15.2 Global frequency ratios for comparisons of concatenated first and second initials

Comparison outcomes (concatenated initials straight-compared, then cross-compared if no straight agreement)	Percentage frequencies		Global frequency ratios (links/non-links)
	Links	Non-links	
Two initials present on both records			
Both agree	57.9	0.2	290/1
One agrees	0.7	5.6	1/8
Neither agrees, both cross-agree	2.4	0.2	12/1
Neither agrees, one cross-agrees*	0.5	4.8	1/10
Neither agrees, no cross-agreement	0.3	31.5	1/105
Two initials on one record, one on the other			
First agrees	4.8	3.3	1.5/1
First disagrees, but cross-agrees*	0.9	3.0	1/3
First disagrees, no cross-agreement	1.0	39.1	1/39
Only the first initial present on each record			
First agrees	31.1	0.9	35/1
First disagrees	0.3	11.2	1/37

*The distinction between the two sorts of cross-agreement (first–second, and second–first) would be made in the case of each such record pair, for the purpose of indicating what cross-comparisons of the remainders of the given names need to be carried out. This would not affect the calculation of the frequency ratios above.

Table 15.3 Specific adjustment factors for male initials

Initial	General frequency* (%)	Specific frequency (%)	Adjustment factor (general/specific frequency)
A	7.30	10.92	0.7
B	7.40	2.26	3.2
C	7.30	5.28	1.4
D	7.30	3.83	1.9
E	7.30	6.57	1.1
F	7.30	4.19	1.7
G	7.30	6.00	1.2
H	7.30	6.40	1.1
I	7.30	0.66	11.0
J	7.30	15.55	0.5
K	7.30	1.00	7.3
L	7.30	4.43	1.7
M	7.30	4.31	1.7
N	7.30	1.64	4.4
O	7.30	1.32	5.6
P	7.30	3.55	2.1
Q	7.30	0.023	217.4
R	7.30	6.56	1.1
S	7.30	3.32	2.2
T	7.30	2.79	2.6
U	7.30	0.12	60.8
V	7.30	0.84	8.7
W	7.30	8.02	0.9
X	7.30	0.07	104.3
Y	7.30	0.25	29.2
Z	7.30	0.10	73.0

*The general frequency is the sum of the squares of all the specific frequencies.

each initial that agreed. Thus, two rare initials that agree will raise the FREQUENCY RATIO by more than just one. Similarly, two common initials that agree will lower it by more than just one. The implementation is simple.

The ADJUSTMENT FACTORS for male initials from a large Canadian file are given in Table 15.3.

16

Comparing and cross-comparing
given names

The manner in which GIVEN NAMES are compared depends on whether one has decided to treat the initials separately from the remainders of the names as just described, or as integral parts of the given names. Either procedure is legitimate. However, the FREQUENCY RATIOS will in the one case be based on the frequencies of the names within the initial that has already been shown to agree, and in the other on the frequencies among all names for that sex. Both procedures give the same end result. The separate FREQUENCY RATIOS for the agreement of an initial and for that of the remainder of the given name, when combined, equal that for the name as a whole. Having indicated the advantages of comparing the initials separately, we confine our discussion here to comparisons of the remainders where the initials have already agreed.

It is a matter of common sense that the sexes be treated separately when dealing both with the initials and the given names. In practice that means creating separate files for the two sexes, and generating separate tables of frequencies and FREQUENCY RATIOS. Only where miscodings of sex are thought to be important would one attempt linkage between records on which the sex disagrees.

Certain logical considerations should govern one's choice of the levels of PARTIAL AGREEMENT that are to be recognized separately when calculating the FREQUENCY RATIOS. If one chooses to recognize differences in the numbers of early characters that agree in a name, it is well to remember that there are three possibilities with respect to the characters that fall beyond the agreement portion:

1. There may be no further characters on either record beyond the agreement portion of the name, i.e. there is FULL AGREEMENT for the name as a whole.
2. The name may be *truncated* on one of the records as compared with the other, beyond the agreement portion, i.e. there is a PARTIAL

AGREEMENT followed by *missing* characters on one of the records, with no actual disagreement of any of the characters.

3. There may be an actual DISAGREEMENT of characters beyond the agreement portion, i.e. there is a PARTIAL AGREEMENT plus a positive DISAGREEMENT.

These three situations are likely to reflect different degrees of certainty even where the numbers of early characters that agree are the same. Subjectively, one would attach more significance to the partial agreement SAM–SAMUEL, than to SAMPSON–SAMUEL, although it is the same number of characters that agree in the two cases. Even greater significance would be attached to the full agreement SAM–SAM, although again it is the same number of characters that agree. This subjective impression is confirmed by the associated FREQUENCY RATIOS.

From this reasoning, a simple rule emerges governing the ways in which one should define the outcome levels to be recognized separately. The rule is: Don't pool the record pairs that relate to these three situations; keep them separate. Within each of the three categories one may, of course, subdivide as finely as one wishes on the basis of the numbers of characters that do agree.

Application of this rule is illustrated in Table 16.1. Certain features of the example require comment.

Table 16.1 Global frequency ratios for different levels of agreement of the remainders of given names — initials already agree (male)

Outcome level	Percentage frequencies Links	Non-links	Global frequency ratios (links/non-links)
No differences			
Full agreement (up to 7 characters)	83.15	13.97	6.0/1
Later characters missing on one record			
First 4 agree + blanks	1.60	0.43	3.7/1
First 3 agree + blanks	0.28	0.20	1.4/1
First 2 agree + blanks	0.04	0.03	1.3/1
Later characters disagree			
First 4 agree + disagreement	4.18	1.21	3.5/1
First 3 agree + disagreement	3.34	2.02	1.7/1
First 2 agree + disagreement	2.23	19.66	1 /8.8
Initial agrees + disagreement	5.15	62.50	1 /12.1

1. The FULL AGREEMENTS have not been subdivided on the basis of the number of characters, but they could be if one wished.
2. There is no category 'initial agrees + blanks' because the FREQUENCY RATIO for this was obtained earlier when the initials were compared separately.
3. The FREQUENCY RATIOS throughout this Table will be less than those for comparisons of whole given names, because they relate just to the frequencies of the remainders of the names, within the initials that have already agreed.
4. These are global FREQUENCY RATIOS. To convert them to their value-specific counterparts they must be adjusted upwards or downwards using the ADJUSTMENT FACTORS for the particular values of the agreement portions of the names.

The data for Table 16.1 relate to straight comparisons only. Where the initials have cross-agreed and the remainders of the names are cross-compared as a result, the likelihood that the remainders will also agree is less than for the corresponding straight comparisons. Thus, separate data are required for all such cross-comparisons.

The conversions to value-specific FREQUENCY RATIOS are illustrated in Table 16.2, using selected male given names with various degrees of truncation. It will be seen from the Table that the ADJUSTMENT FACTORS for initials plus remainders combined (final set of columns) are the products of those for the initials alone and remainders alone.

Such tables may use percentage frequencies, as above, or logarithms of the frequencies. With the logarithms, of course, the ADJUSTMENT FACTOR becomes an ADJUSTMENT WEIGHT which is added to, or subtracted from, the weight representing the FREQUENCY RATIO. The end result is the same with either usage.

Other comparison schemes might make use of phonetic codings of the given names. The best guide in such matters is careful visual examination of the name pairs that fail to agree fully in linked pairs of records, plus empirical testing of any proposed comparison schemes on these discrepant names. Success may be measured in terms of the extent to which the machine is rendered capable of recognizing the name similarities that are apparent to a human.

Ideally, of course, one might even recognize the full specificities of the more common combinations of synonyms and near synonyms. This is possible but requires data from large numbers of linked pairs.

Table 16.2 Specific frequencies and adjustment factors for initials and given names (male)

Name (full or truncated)	Initial alone			Remainder alone			Whole name		
	General frequency (%)	Specific frequency (%)	Adjustment factor (general/specific)	General frequency (%)	Specific frequency (%)	Adjustment factor (general/specific)	General frequency (%)	Specific frequency (%)	Adjustment factor (general/specific)
WILLIAM	7.30	8.02	0.9	14.29	57.43	0.3	1.043	4.606	0.3
WILL	7.30	8.02	0.9	16.05	61.58	0.3	1.172	4.939	0.3
WIL	7.30	8.02	0.9	18.32	61.58	0.3	1.337	4.939	0.3
WI	7.30	8.02	0.9	32.86	70.71	0.5	2.399	5.671	0.5
W	7.30	8.02	0.9	100.00	100.00	1.0	7.300	8.020	0.9
ZACKARY	7.30	0.10	73.0	14.29	0.20	71.5	1.043	0.00020	5215.0
ZACK	7.30	0.10	73.0	16.05	0.84	19.1	1.172	0.00084	1395.2
ZAC	7.30	0.10	73.0	18.32	10.15	1.8	1.337	0.01015	131.7
ZA	7.30	0.10	73.0	32.86	15.39	2.1	2.399	0.01539	155.9
Z	7.30	0.10	73.0	100.00	100.00	1.0	7.300	0.10000	73.0

17

Comparing years of birth

Comparisons of the YEAR OF BIRTH are treated separately from the corresponding comparisons of the month and day of birth. This is because the distribution of the years of birth on a file is unlikely to be uniform over time. As well, the distributions will probably differ for any two files that are being linked. This complicates calculation of the frequencies of various levels of AGREEMENT and PARTIAL AGREEMENT in randomly matched pairs of records. With a flow of routine linkage jobs involving different files, the calculation is therefore unlikely to be done separately for each job, even though this ought to be the case. However, this tedious calculation becomes unnecessary where a real file of UNLINKABLE pairs has already been created as a source of other frequencies for the denominators of the FREQUENCY RATIOS.

The fineness with which one should divide the outcome levels for PARTIAL AGREEMENTS and more extreme DISAGREEMENTS is best determined by starting with a much larger number of levels than is thought necessary. Those yielding similar FREQUENCY RATIOS may then be recombined to reduce the number. The example in

Table 17.1 Frequency ratios for different levels of agreement of year of birth

Outcome level (difference in years, + or −	Percentage frequencies		Frequency ratios (links/ non-links)
	Links	Non-links	
FULL AGREEMENT	77.3	1.1	72/1
Difference = 1 year	15.1	2.2	7/1
Difference = 2–3 years	3.9	4.2	1/1
Difference = 4–6 years	2.5	6.4	1/3
Difference = 7–10 years	0.6	8.9	1/15
Difference = 11 + years	0.7	77.2	1/115

Table 17.1 is a product of such prior testing, and is based on an actual file of UNLINKABLE pairs.

As a simple rule of thumb, differences of twofold or more in the FREQUENCY RATIOS may be considered worth recognizing separately. In Table 17.1, most adjacent levels differ by from five- to tenfold. This represents reasonably good use of the discriminating power of the identifier, but the best possible use would require a still finer breakdown.

It is not proposed here that the comparison also be made value specific for the calendar period, for example for decade of birth. This would be possible, however, where there is a logical reason for such a distinction. One possible good reason is discussed later in connection with the calculation of ABSOLUTE OVERALL ODDS in favour of a true linkage.

18

Comparing and cross-comparing months and days of birth

The MONTH and the DAY OF BIRTH on a matched pair of records may be compared directly, and they may also be cross-compared if they disagree and are suspected of having been inverted.

Straight comparisons of the month and the day of birth are usually simpler than those of year of birth. Because the births themselves are more or less uniformly distributed over the months of the year and the days of the month, it is relatively easy to calculate how often various levels of AGREEMENT and PARTIAL AGREEMENT are likely to occur by chance. In an actual file of UNLINKABLE pairs the frequencies of the different outcome levels are, in fact, much as one would expect.

As with the comparison of year of birth, it is best to start by recog-

Table 18.1 Frequency ratios for different levels of agreement of day and month of birth

Outcome level (difference in days or months, + or −	Percentage frequencies		Frequency ratios (links/ non-links)
	Links	Non-links	
DAY OF BIRTH			
FULL AGREEMENT	85.1	3.3	25.8/1
Difference = 1 day	4.5	6.3	1 /1.4
Difference = 2–3 days	2.0	12.2	1 /6.1
Difference = 4–9 days	4.5	31.1	1 /6.9
Difference = 10+ days	3.9	47.1	1 /12.1
MONTH OF BIRTH			
FULL AGREEMENT	93.3	8.3	11.2/1
Difference = 1 month	3.6	15.4	1 /4.3
Difference = 2 months	0.8	14.1	1 /17.6
Difference = 3+ months	2.3	62.2	1 /27.0

nizing more levels of outcome than are thought to be necessary. Then, those levels which are found to have similar FREQUENCY RATIOS may be recombined with each other without significant loss of discriminating power. The examples given in Table 18.1 are products of this approach.

If frequent inversions of the month and day are suspected, one may wish to *cross-compare* these identifiers where they both disagree on straight comparison. Current practice in the matter is arbitrary and the FREQUENCY RATIOS it yields are probably not appropriate. What is actually done, after carrying out the straight comparisons of the month and the day of birth as shown in Table 18.1, is to follow this with a separate cross-comparison step wherever there is no straight agreement of either. The problem with this approach is that the FREQUENCY RATIOS from the latter are not independent of those from the former and the two cannot be appropriately combined. Neither can one correctly cancel out the evidence from the straight disagreement when it is followed by a cross-agreement, as has sometimes been done in the past.

The best course is probably to do as was indicated for the initials, and combine the straight and cross-comparisons into a single comparison procedure. This option reduces somewhat the number of levels of PARTIAL AGREEMENT that it is convenient to recognize, but the compromise may well be tolerable where the cross-agreements are common. Table 18.2 contains an example of this approach. The data in the Table relate to the linkage of two work files, in at least one of which the dates of birth were obviously inaccurately recorded.

There is an added advantage in combining all the outcomes from both the straight and the cross-comparisons into a single comparison procedure. Not only does this solve the problem of correctly combining the FREQUENCY RATIOS from the two sorts of comparison. But, in addition, disagreements of the month and day of birth are known to occur together more often than would be expected on chance, and the bias from this source is best avoided through concatenating the correlated identifiers when comparing them.

Table 18.2 Frequency ratios for comparisons and cross-comparisons of day (D) and month (M) of birth where different levels of agreement are taken into account

MM	DD	MD	DM	(differences in months or days, for comparisons and cross-comparisons)	Links	Non-links	Frequency ratios (links/ non-links)
0	0	—	—	(both agree)	40.25	0.27	149.1/1
0	1	—	—	(M agrees, D partial)	4.45	0.57	7.8/1
0	2-3	—	—	(M agrees, D partial)	3.73	1.06	3.5/1
0	4+	—	—	(M agrees, D disagrees)	22.30	6.51	3.4/1
1	0	—	—	(M partial, D agrees)	1.46	0.19	7.7/1
2-3	0	—	—	(M partial, D agrees)	4.44	0.67	6.6/1
4+	0	—	—	(M disagrees, D agrees)	3.73	1.43	2.6/1
1+	1+	0	0	(M cross-agrees, D cross-agrees)	0.37	2.04	1 /5.5
1+	1+	0	1+	(M cross-agrees, D cross-disagrees)	0.75	2.98	1 /4.0
1+	1+	1+	0	(M cross-disagrees, D cross-agrees)	1.40	2.98	1 /2.1
1+	1+	1+	1+	(M cross-disagrees, D cross-disagrees)	17.12	81.30	1 /4.7

Outcome levels (differences in months or days, for comparisons and cross-comparisons); Percentage frequencies: Links, Non-links

19

Comparing places of birth

Comparisons of PLACES OF BIRTH, when linking with Canadian vital registrations, have usually recognized only the simple agreement and disagreement outcomes. However, there are circumstances in which more sophisticated comparison procedures are required. Sometimes the codes for province or foreign country of birth may differ but still indicate partial agreement. Another sort of complication occurs where the codes for two or more family members are available for comparison but are apt to be correlated with each other.

The simple agreement/disagreement outcomes require only straightforward treatment. There are 99 two-digit codes in all. A separate code is assigned to each Canadian province or territory (codes 1–12) and there is also a code for 'Canada' (code 17), which indicates that the province is unknown. The remaining codes are grouped so that the first digit has some significance on its own as indicated below.

Codes	Country or group of countries
21–26	England, N. Ireland, Ireland, Scotland, Wales, Lesser Isles;
31–37	Australia, New Zealand, S. and S.W. Africa, other former British Africa, India and Pakistan, other former British Asia, other former British;
41–45	USA, Mexico, other N. America, Central America, South America;
51–59	Albania, Austria, Belgium, Bulgaria, Czechoslovakia, Denmark, Estonia, Finland, France;
60–69	Germany, Greece, Holland, Hungary, Iceland, Italy, Latvia, Lithuania, Norway, Poland;
70–77	Portugal, Romania, Spain, Sweden, Switzerland, Yugoslavia, other Europe, USSR;
82–86	China, Japan, Syria, Turkey, other Asia;
91–98	Africa (not former British), other countries, Palestine/Israel, at sea.

The actual names of some of the countries covered by the codes have changed with time, so the codes themselves are often easier to use in a linkage operation than the alphabetical names would be.

The frequencies of these codes in the Canadian death records are given in tables, and similar tables would not be difficult to prepare from census data for the living population. Since men tend to be more mobile than women the frequencies will differ for the two sexes, sometimes substantially.

A need to recognize PARTIAL AGREEMENTS sometimes arises where a record with the code for 'Canada' is compared with a record bearing the code of a particular Canadian province. Whatever comparison procedure is devised to deal with this could be applicable also to other instances in which the codes 'partially' disagree, for example with respect to the second digit only. Whether such refinements are needed is best determined by looking at the discrepant pairs of codes that actually occur in the LINKED pairs of records. Details of a possible comparison procedure that recognizes more than one level of agreement are indicated in Table 19.1. These are essentially global FREQUENCY RATIOS, which would subsequently be converted to their value-specific counterparts with the aid of a look-up table of ADJUSTMENT FACTORS.

One final problem concerns comparisons involving the places of birth of two or more family members. Death records and birth records frequently contain not only the place of birth of the individual registrant but also those of the parents. Similarly, pension records may contain the place of birth of the registrant plus those of

Table 19.1 Frequency ratios for different levels of agreement of place of birth

Outcome levels	Percentage frequencies		Frequency ratios (links/ non-links)
	Links	Non-links	
Full agreement (both digits agree)	86.93	11.77	7.4/1
'Canada' vs. a Canadian province (code 17 vs codes 1–12)	0.65	2.21	1 /3.4
Other partial agreement/disagreement (first digit 2 + and agrees, second disagrees)	0.82	3.46	1 /4.2
Disagreement (excluding the above)	11.60	82.56	1 /7.1

the spouse and any children born to the couple. Thus, more than one place of birth may be available for comparison in a pair of records when linking any of these files with each other.

The problem is best illustrated with an example. Consider a matched pair of records in which both the husband and the wife were born in, say, China. The place of birth of the husband will obviously carry considerable discriminating power when it agrees. But the further agreement of the wife's place of birth adds little to our assurance of a correct match. This would be intuitively obvious to a manual searcher. However, if the wife had been born in a different country, say Switzerland, a double agreement of the two different places of birth would substantially increase the level of assurance. There is need for a sensible set of guidelines to handle such situations, as relating to two or even three places of birth of family members. The following rules may be applied to a given record pair:

1. Calculate the FREQUENCY RATIO for the PLACE OF BIRTH comparison with respect to the husband first. If the outcome is an agreement, ignore any further agreements with respect to that particular province or foreign country.
2. Calculate the FREQUENCY RATIO for the PLACE OF BIRTH comparison with respect to the wife next, but discard it if it duplicates a previous agreement with respect to the husband's place of birth.
3. Calculate the FREQUENCY RATIO for the place of birth comparison with respect to the offspring next, but discard it if it duplicates a previous agreement with respect to the place of birth of either the husband or the wife.

(If it proved necessary, the above rules could even be reworded to deal similarly with the FREQUENCY RATIOS for any duplicate *disagreements*, i.e. those disagreements in which the discrepant place ⟶ place of birth combinations are the same for two or more family members.)

These precautions against calculating unjustifiably high levels of assurance have been found to be essential when linking into sibship groupings the birth records pertaining to racial minorities. For example, in the absence of such rules, a birth record for an ethnic Chinese child in Canada is apt to link falsely, but with seemingly great assurance, into many different sibships that are ethnic Chinese.

20

Comparing other geographical identifiers

The other most frequently used geographical identifiers are the PLACES of RESIDENCE, WORK, and DEATH. For a death search it is usual to compare the place of work as indicated on a work record, with the place of residence or of death as indicated on a death record. Sometimes the number of useful outcome levels or values from such comparisons is small enough to be written directly into the instructions to the computer. Alternatively it may be desirable to recognize larger numbers of outcomes so that look-up tables are needed and a conversion step to a higher level of specificity is involved.

The basis of any such comparison procedure is, again, a matter of common sense plus empirical testing; in other words, first do some manual linking to see what combinations of places of work versus places of death are likely. Many workers die at or near the community in which they were employed. Others will move elsewhere to retire and later die. Some will move to a new job first. Where changes of residence occur there will often be 'fashionable' patterns of migration, for example westward in Canada for retirement or to another mining or manufacturing district for a new job. For employees of a company with widely distributed sites of operation, each site may be associated with quite different patterns of migration on retirement. For workers who have particular kinds of jobs, the migration to new employment may be selectively to localities in which there are similar industries. A typical comparison procedure is shown in Table 20.1.

The reader will be aware that the distinction between a 'global' and a 'value-specific' FREQUENCY RATIO may become very much a matter of degree in many such situations. It is often convenient to incorporate some limited specificity for field value into the compact set of instructions that are given directly to the computer, but more may be desirable from a less compact external source. For example, where a number of different work sites in the same province have

Table 20.1 Frequency ratios for place of work versus place of death, for workers at widely separated sites

Outcome levels (place of death)	Percentage frequencies		Frequency ratio (links/ non-links)
	Links	Non-links	
Workers at a western (Alberta) site			
Same district as place of work	5.52	0.28	19.7/1
Edmonton, Alberta	18.62	2.41	7.7/1
Other Alberta–British Columbia	35.17	18.62	1.9/1
Manitoba–Saskatchewan	13.10	8.28	1.6/1
Ontario	20.69	35.86	1 /1.7
Quebec–Atlantic provinces	5.52	36.55	1 /6.6
Workers at an eastern (Ontario) site			
Same city as place of work	33.90	0.08	423.8/1
Other Ontario	74.58	35.59	2.1/1
Alberta–British Columbia	20.34	18.64	1.1/1
Manitoba–Saskatchewan	5.08	8.47	1 /1.1
Quebec–Atlantic provinces	8.47	37.29	1 /4.4

been grouped for the purposes of defining a given outcome level, look-up tables of ADJUSTMENT FACTORS for agreements with respect to particular cities or regions could then be used to carry out the conversions of the relevant FREQUENCY RATIO(S) to a higher level of specificity.

The process of thus converting to higher levels of specificity is made tidy and simple where all of the frequencies dealt with relate to defined outcomes in *pairs* of records, as distinct from the frequencies of particular values in files of single, i.e. *unpaired*, records.

21

Comparing marital status

The discriminating power of MARITAL STATUS as an identifier depends less on the agreements than on the fact that the status is more apt to progress forward than backwards. People do not normally become 'single' again once they have been 'married'. When a marriage ends, the next state is correctly called something other than 'single'. For simplicity we use the term 'was married' to include 'divorced', 'widowed', and also 'separated' where this is reported on a form.

If good use is to be made of the discriminating power of MARITAL STATUS, at least nine levels of outcome should be recognized. Some of these are likely to be rare among the correctly LINKED pairs of records, because when they do occur it is as a result of incorrect reporting or coding. The proposed comparison procedure for a death search is illustrated in Table 21.1.

Table 21.1 Frequency ratios for marital status on a work record versus a death record

Outcome levels		Percentage frequencies		Frequency ratios
Status on work record	Status on death record	Links	Non-links	(links/ non-links)
Single	Single	60.81	29.2	2.1/1
Single	Married	32.56	57.1	1 /1.8
Single	Was married	6.61	13.7	1 /2.1
Married	Single	4.82	29.2	1 /6.1
Married	Married	78.66	57.1	1.4/1
Married	Was married	16.52	13.7	1.2/1
Was married	Single	19.23	29.2	1 /1.5
Was married	Married	26.92	57.1	1 /2.1
Was married	Was married	53.85	13.7	4.2/1

Where finer distinctions are available in the records being linked (e.g. between 'separated', 'widowed', and 'divorced') there is no reason why use should not be made of the added discriminating power. The number of outcome levels will be increased, but no great labour is involved in writing the additional lines of instructions to the computer. The likely outcome frequencies and FREQUENCY RATIOS will not be known initially but these can be left blank at the outset. They will be filled in later, after a preliminary file of LINKED pairs of records has been obtained and a comparison file of UNLINKABLE pairs has been set up.

Other refinements are possible. For example, the likelihood of a change in marital status will vary with the sex and age of the individual, and with the interval of time between creation of the earlier and the later record of a matched pair. Usually the FREQUENCY RATIOS will be made specific only for sex, but there is no reason why separate tables of FREQUENCY RATIOS could not be prepared for different age-ranges and for longer versus shorter time periods. As with most potential refinements, it is the pay-off in terms of increased discriminating power that should determine how much effort will be devoted to the development work. A useful refinement, however, may be used repeatedly.

In general, wherever a human searcher has found such a distinction helpful in visually resolving difficult or borderline links, the same distinction will often be worth incorporating into the comparison procedure used by the computer. This generalization is as applicable to marital status as to any other identifier.

22

Using other identifiers

A number of identifiers that have not been discussed so far deserve
brief mention because of their ability to serve special purposes.
These include the year in which an individual was last known to have
been alive, the Canadian Social Insurance Number (SIN) or its
equivalent in other countries, the coded cause of death, and various
family identifiers. These have been used to improve the efficiency of
searching and linking, to establish that individuals are still alive, and
to create family groupings of health records.

The *year last known alive* (YRLKA) is commonly determined
from the last of a set of work records. If this is trusted to be correct,
death searches prior to the YRLKA may be avoided. Alternatively,
the death searches may include all years of death, with the YRLKA
being used to indicate apparent conflicts that require visual
inspection.

The Canadian *Social Insurance Number* (SIN) is rarely reported
on death records but is commonly available on work records. It may
be used to extract the relatively high-quality identifiers that are contained in the Index of Social Insurance Numbers, so that these can be
employed in the death searches. It is capable of serving to verify that
an individual is still alive, through linkage with active files pertaining
to living people, such as those of the federal taxation office, the
Canada Pension Plan, Old Age Security and Guaranteed Income
Supplement, and the provincial records of persons over age 65 who
are eligible for free drugs. Similar uses are possible for the personal
identity numbers of other countries, and there is an additional use
for death searching wherever such numbers are present on the death
registrations as with the US Social Security Number.

The coded *cause of death* on death registrations may be used as
linking information where death searches are initiated by the records
of special disease registers which likewise contain *diagnoses*, as when
carrying out 'death clearance' of cancer registers.

Family identifiers are included in all of the vital registrations.

These may be used to improve the linkage of records pertaining to individuals, as when infant death records are linked to the relevant birth records. They may also serve to establish sibship groupings of birth records, to which can be added the parental marriage records, the death records of the siblings, and other health records. The family identifiers contained in the marriage records are of even greater interest, because these make it possible to expand the sibship groupings into networks of related sibships. This is because the marriage registration contains three surname pairs, relating respectively to the parents of the groom, the parents of the bride, and the newly married couple themselves. A given marriage record may therefore be entered into three locations in a file that is sequenced by the male plus female surname pairs. There is a considerable body of experience in such uses of family identifiers, based on the vital and health records for the Canadian province of British Columbia.

The comparison procedures for these additional identifiers are likely to be much the same as those described earlier.

23

Updating the numerators and denominators of the frequency ratios

When starting a new linkage job it is frequently convenient to make use initially of FREQUENCY RATIOS based on NUMERATORS and DENOMINATORS that were obtained in the course of a previous job. These will not always be strictly appropriate, but they will ensure that some experience is gained quickly with the new files. Before a final production run, however, the numerators for all the identifier comparisons should be updated, and so also should some of the corresponding denominators.

Updating the NUMERATORS is conceptually an iterative process. The first file of LINKED pairs to be obtained is viewed as imperfect because it is based on numerators from an unrelated file of LINKED pairs. The idea is that new numerators may now be obtained from this first file of LINKED pairs. The result on a next round of relinkage will be an improved but still imperfect second file of LINKED pairs, and so on until significant further improvement is no longer likely. In practice, the process is usually shortened to a single relinkage. This is possible because manual resolutions of the relatively small numbers of borderline links in the first file of LINKED pairs result in numerators that are unlikely to be improved on later.

Updating the DENOMINATORS is a different matter because conceptually they are based on a file of randomly matched UNLINKABLE pairs that can be assembled at any time. Also, if we were to assume that the file initiating the searches is essentially similar to the file being searched, updating would not be required for each new job. However, this may not be even approximately true with respect to such characteristics as the use of shortened versions of the given names, the availabilities of middle names or initials, and the frequencies of the different forms of marital status and different years of birth. As a result, at least some of the denominators do need to be updated for many of the new jobs. This is likely to be the case for the comparison procedures relating to INITIALS, GIVEN

NAMES, YEARS OF BIRTH, GEOGRAPHICAL IDENTIFIERS, and MARITAL STATUS.

Where a file of UNLINKABLE pairs is produced routinely, updating the DENOMINATORS should present no problem. However, where such a file is not created routinely, and where new denominators can only be obtained by recalculating them each time there is a new job, the calculation is likely to be neglected. As a result, old and inappropriate denominators are apt to be used repeatedly. This is just one of the reasons for favouring the routine creation of an actual file of UNLINKABLE pairs.

24

Flexibility in the use of files of linked and unlinkable pairs

Information required for calculating the FREQUENCY RATIOS ought to be readily extractable from the LINKED pairs of records, and by identical methods from the UNLINKABLE pairs as well. Over and above this, there is the need to test possible alternative rules for the comparison procedures. This would be accomplished most simply by extracting the same kind of information from the same sources, but in the variant forms specified by the alternative outcome definitions.

For a given set of rules and for each of the resulting levels of outcome, what are required are the *counts*, the *percentage frequencies* (either excluding the 'missing' values from the calculation, or not, as appropriate), and the *logarithms* of the frequencies (preferably to the base 2, and possibly multiplied by 10 to avoid decimals). These should be obtainable from both the LINKED and the UNLINKABLE pairs.

It is not really sufficient that this 'outcome information' be obtained only for the comparison rules actually used in the prior provisional linkages. If improvements are to be made, any proposed changes need to be seen to be worth while. For example, the groupings of outcome levels should not combine, in the same group, components which separately would have had FREQUENCY RATIOS differing by much more than twofold. This would be wasteful of discriminating power. But only a finer breakdown of the outcome levels will enable one to determine whether such inappropriate pooling had actually occurred.

A similar need for flexibility arises where the place of work is to be compared with the place of death. One cannot be sure in advance which combinations of places will produce which levels of discrimination, in a positive or in a negative sense. Current practice involves a trial-and-error process, requiring data for various combinations of places to be extracted by separate tabulation and to be manipulated manually, prior to pooling those combinations that yield similar FREQUENCY RATIOS. The relevant facts, however, are all contained in the two files of matched pairs once these have been established. Flexibility in the extraction of the information according to a diversity of comparison rules and outcome definitions is what is needed. Only thus can decisions about the 'best' comparison procedure be reached objectively.

In general, such flexibility is desirable when testing various possible rules for the comparison of almost any identifier. The need arises because available discriminating power is only put to best use through recognition of the appropriate multiple levels of outcome. Visual matching may provide initial insights, but relevant data are needed to eliminate guesswork.

The ultimate purpose is for the computer to adopt the strategies of the human mind in order to keep expensive clerical resolutions to a minimum.

25

Some pitfalls

There are pitfalls for the unwary, and sources of confusion that have probably been felt at some time by all who have done this sort of work. Mostly, trouble arises when one stops thinking in terms of the FREQUENCY RATIOS. These are indeed ratios, and it is best if decisions are not based on NUMERATORS or DENOMINATORS alone. Another potential source of confusion is sometimes unnecessary separation of two related steps in a comparison that would be better carried out as a single procedure. Some examples are now given.

At one stage in the work on record linkage, it became routine practice to base the early rejections of unpromising candidate pairs of records wholly on the accumulation of unusually small NUMERATORS (the logarithms of which were termed 'transmission weights'). The corresponding DENOMINATORS were ignored. Eventually the procedure yielded obvious nonsense and was abandoned in favour of one which took both components of the RATIO into account. This confusion may have arisen because all logarithms were called 'weights' whether they pertained to a ratio, or just an orphaned component of a ratio.

A more recent incorrect practice has been to cancel out, or discard, the unfavourable ODDS or FREQUENCY RATIOS resulting from disagreements of the two initials, when these are later shown to cross-agree. An earlier and similarly incorrect alternative was to retain the whole of these unfavourable ODDS. Both practices are wrong, as a simple test will show; and it will be intuitively obvious that failure on a first try followed by success on a second is not the same as success on the first. Although the error cannot exceed the magnitude of the ODDS arising from the original straight disagreements, those ODDS will be large where the initials are accurately reported in both of the files being linked. A guesswork solution is in any case unnecessary and best avoided.

Other kinds of conditional comparison steps run into a similar problem. This is not because it is inherently wrong to do the related comparisons in more than one step, but merely because it is confusing, and particularly so where the elements of the appropriate FREQUENCY RATIOS are not both readily available as actual measurements. As well, the single-step multiple-outcome procedures have the special advantage of a built-in safeguard; when correctly done, the combined frequencies of all outcomes should add up to 100 per cent, among both the LINKED and the UNLINKABLE pairs.

A further kind of confusion surrounds the use of calculated DENOMINATORS. In simple situations there is little problem even with the PARTIAL AGREEMENTS, and in more complicated situations the theory appears to be adequate. The real problem is that of translating the theoretical solutions into a daily routine that will be correctly applied in a flexible manner to a succession of diverse linkage jobs. The problem is solved by constructing an actual file of UNLINKABLE pairs, drawn from the files that are being linked. However, this empirical solution is only gradually coming into routine use.

There is one general rule for clearing one's own mind whenever a confusing point is under discussion: return to the ODDS or FREQUENCY RATIO formula and do most empirical tests manually. This might mean carrying out a few difficult linkages visually. Or it might involve scanning real files of LINKED and UNLINKABLE pairs to extract on a small scale the NUMERATORS and DENOMINATORS (i.e. the outcome frequencies among the links and the non-links) that are strictly relevant to the question at issue. The approach is well worth the tedium, and the result is sometimes both satisfying and exciting.

Finally, readers familiar with the complexity of the more formal statements of linkage theory may wonder whether the present FREQUENCY RATIO formula represents an over-simplification. It does not. The following are omitted:

(1) the *logarithms*, which are merely a device for doing the multiplications and divisions, and are irrelevant to the theory;
(2) the calculations and assumptions by which the DENOMINATORS in the FREQUENCY RATIOS are estimated when not available directly from files of UNLINKABLE pairs, since such calculations can be handled separately when needed;
(3) prior decisions on whether the outcome frequencies among the LINKED

and UNLINKABLE pairs are to be based on all such pairs, or on a defined subset (e.g. in which an identifier is always present, or in which the search record carries a specified value), since such decisions should in any case depend on the particular application.

These deliberate omissions serve to emphasize the essentially obvious nature of the linkage rationale. When actually applying the theory, it seems that all of us need to visualize it intuitively if we are to keep a clear head and avoid pitfalls.

Part III

Saving central processor time

26

Staging the refinements

If one had to compare in detail every record in a file initiating a search, against every record in the file being searched, linkage would be impracticably time consuming for any but very small files. This is true whether the task is automated or manual.

To avoid such unnecessary work, crude methods of comparison that consume little time are used first to exclude the majority of the candidate pairs for linkage. These are followed by comparisons of increasing refinement. The most sophisticated procedures, which also use the most time, are reserved until the end when the numbers of pairs to be examined has been greatly reduced.

Such staging in the use of increasing degees of refinements is common practice for the human searcher, and should be copied in any automated equivalent. The following steps have become a commonplace part of the overall strategy:

1. Avoid creating the great majority of the potentially possible comparison pairs, through file 'blocking'. For manual searching this usually means the use of an alphabetical sequence under surname. For computer searching a phonetically coded form of the surname (e.g. the N Y S I I S code) is commonly employed instead. Comparisons are normally made only within blocks.

2. For the record pairs that are created, start by comparing a few key identifiers briefly to see if there are any agreements at all. A human searcher will normally check the initials; the computer may check the date of birth as well. If there is no agreement of any element of the key identifiers the comparison is apt to stop there. The pair is not examined further.

3. For the remaining pairs, all available identifiers common to a pair are then compared. Simple comparisons are made in this stage, and more importance is attached to names and dates of birth than to other less discriminating identifiers such as province of residence. But the particular name or place that agrees may be ignored. A further elimination of obviously unlinkable pairs occurs here whether the search is clerical or automated.

4. For the pairs that have survived the previous hurdles, the comparisons

will now be more detailed and time consuming. Special attention is given to whether the names, places of residence and such, are rare or common. Account is taken of the greater discriminating power of the agreements where the identifiers have rare 'values' as compared with those of their more common counterparts. Again, this is the way in which the human mind works and it is equally appropriate for the computer.

In all of the above steps, the aim is to reduce the burden of applying refined criteria at a stage when cruder and less time-consuming rules are sufficient. The success at each stage, and the cost, may be measured in terms of the factor reduction in candidate pairs for linkage, as against the effort required to achieve that reduction and the numbers of potential good links that may have been inadvertently discarded with the bad ones.

Typical magnitudes of the reduction factors at each stage are given in Table 26.1.

Where a computer has done the linking, the further refinement of a manual check may be limited to a minute fraction of the remaining candidate pairs for linkage. The pairs are first arrayed in descending order of the calculated OVERALL ODDS in favour of a correct link. Visual inspection is then required only for those pairs with border-line degrees of assurance. The purpose of the various refinements in the comparison procedures described in Part II has been to reduce to a minimum this potentially expensive manual–clerical step.

Some of the practical details of these steps are discussed in Chapter 27.

Table 26.1 Numbers of candidate pairs for linkage at different stages in the elimination process (assuming 50 000 search records, 2 000 000 death records, and 20 000 correct links)

Stage in the elimination process	Pairs remaining	Stage reduction factor
Before any blocking	100 000 000 000	—
1. After surname blocking (by NYSIIS)	80 000 000	1,250/1
2. After preliminary rejections (no agreement in initials or date of birth)	16 000 000	5/1
3. After value non-specific comparisons	40 000	400/1
4. After value-specific comparisons (plus possible manual checking of difficult cases)	20 000	2/1

27

Details of the eliminations

It would not be far wrong to view record linkage as a process of attrition. Initially there is a potentially massive number of record pairs, few of which are correctly matched. The process of separating out the true matches is in reality a stepwise elimination of the false ones. It is not so much a matter of picking needles out of a haystack, as of progressively getting rid of the haystack without losing the needles.

The biggest role played by the identifying information is not one of singling out the good matches, but rather of identifying the bad ones. If we were to start by ignoring all the identifiers, the potential number of candidate pairs for linkage would be the product of the numbers of records in the two files that are being linked. As increasing amounts of the identifying information are brought into play, a stepwise narrowing down of the remaining candidate pairs occurs through the successive eliminations of 'failed pairs'.

We now consider the practical details of four principle steps in this elimination process:

(1) BLOCKING the files;
(2) the *preliminary rejections*,
(3) the *comparison sequence* and its *early cut-off*;
(4) the application of *value-specific* DISCRIMINATING POWER.

The implementation of these steps is discussed in the Sections that follow.

27.1. Blocking the files

It is common practice to sequence the files for a linkage operation by a phonetically coded version of the surname. The N Y S I I S code is well suited for this. It carries greater discriminating power than another popular code, the Soundex, and it is reasonably efficient in bringing together variant spellings of the same names.

A frequent mistake, when making minor changes in such codes with a view to improving their efficiency, is to miss the main point of the coding. The object is not simply to bring together the variant forms of a name, nor to retain a high level of discriminating power. Rather, the purpose is to achieve an optimum trade-off between the two. The efficiency of a code is best measured in terms of this trade-off.

Wherever there is a real need to capture the linkages that are missed because of such a code, the most productive tactic is often to make a second search under an alternative sequence. The most effective alternative sequence is likely to be by the first given name followed by the date of birth, or vice versa. Even where these identifiers are inaccurately reported they should still bring together a substantial proportion of the potential true links that have been missed under the phonetic code alone.

The essence of the NYSIIS code is the conversion of the more labile groups of letters in a name, into standardized alternatives (e.g. the first letters 'MAC' to 'MCC', 'KN' to 'NN', 'SCH' to 'SSS', and subsequent letter 'SCH' to 'SSA', 'PH' to 'FF', and so on). All vowels are changed to the single letter 'A', and some of the final letters are converted (e.g. 'AY' to 'Y') or deleted (e.g. 'S' and 'A').

The ability of the NYSIIS code to divide a file finely may be measured by summing the squares of the frequencies of the various 'values' of the code in that file. For a file of Canadian death records the resulting 'general' frequency is 0.087 per cent. This means that the degree of fineness to which the file is broken up by the code is, for practical purposes, the same as if it had been equally divided into 1148 blocks each representing 0.087 per cent of the file. With the full alphabetical surnames the corresponding figures would be 2284 blocks each representing 0.044 per cent of the file. So the power to divide the file is reduced by the coding by a factor of two.

The NYSIIS code is recommended as the blocking agent for most linkage operations. It is known to differ about 2 per cent of the time in pairs of records brought together by the Canadian SIN and believed to be correctly linked, although the figure may vary with the proportions of foreign names. Where a 2 per cent loss of potential good links due to blocking is too high, multiple alternative searching sequences may provide the most promising approach.

27.2. The preliminary rejections

Record pairs created within the file blocks are best subjected to a simple first test, prior to initiating the full comparison sequence. A test that has worked particularly well uses five main identifiers:

(1) first initial;
(2) second initial;
(3) year of birth;
(4) month of birth;
(5) day of birth.

Where no full agreement is found in any of these, the record pair is judged unlinkable and is rejected.

This test has come to be known as the 'tough' rule for the *preliminary rejections*, to distinguish it from various watered-down versions of the rule. The procedure has been found to reduce the early mass of unlinkable candidate pairs by a factor of between five- and sixfold. There is also reason to believe that it will not lose as many as one per thousand of the potential good links. The saving in central processor time and costs should be substantial, because (a) no FREQUENCY RATIOS need be calculated, (b) the number of identifiers compared is small, and (c) only two outcomes need be recognized — 'agree' and 'disagree or missing'.

'Softer' versions of the rejection rule have been less successful. These are sometimes employed because of fear of losing a good link, but the factor reduction is considerably less. One such version requires that all five identifiers positively disagree before the pair is rejected. However, this allows all record pairs with any missing identifier among the five to remain, including all with a missing middle initial. As a result, the reduction is apt to be in the vicinity of only twofold.

An 'intermediate' rule that allows the initials to be cross-compared in a search for the one positive agreement that would rescue the record pair, may be an attractive compromise. The additional unlinkable pairs that will thereby escape the preliminary rejection are not excessive. For example, where both initials are present, one of them is apt to cross-agree by chance about 14 per cent of the time; this would lessen a sixfold reduction, but only to about fivefold.

It is recommended that the preliminary rejections use either the 'tough' rule or the 'intermediate' version. The 'soft' rule is too permissive where 'missing' identifiers are common.

27.3. The comparison sequence and its early cut-off

The *comparison sequence* for the full complement of identifiers follows, and is based on the global FREQUENCY RATIOS. However, it may be interrupted by an *early cut-off* where the record pair is quickly seen to be unlinkable.

The idea of the cut-off is to save central processor time by aborting the comparison sequence as soon as the accumulated ODDS or FREQUENCY RATIOS become excessively unfavourable. The logical point at which to stop is where even complete agreement of all remaining identifiers could not reverse the unfavourable RATIO. This ploy will reduce the number of comparison steps, but usually by less than a factor of two.

To make the early cut-off work, one calculates the global FREQUENCY RATIOS for the full agreement of each of the identifiers. At any given point in the comparison sequence, the maximum collective favourable ODDS that could still be accumulated from that point towards will indicate what improvement in the overall ODDS might conceivably result if the comparisons were continued.

A fixed threshold is implied for the complete accumulated FREQUENCY RATIO. Less favourable accumulated RATIOS might be tolerated at an intermediate stage, but only where the remaining steps continued to hold some prospect of restoring the balance to the level acceptable at the end. The setting of this threshold is discussed later (p. 91). The extent to which the intermediate accumulated FREQUENCY RATIOS would be allowed to drop below that threshold is indicated by the penultimate column of Table 27.1. The final column shows how rapidly the unfavourable FREQUENCY RATIOS could conceivably accumulate. The early cut-off point will depend on what threshold is chosen for the combined ODDS from the complete comparison sequence.

27.4. The application of value-specific discriminating powers

For reasons of economy the first series of identifier comparisons is

Table 27.1 Basis of an early cut-off procedure

Identifier	Frequency ratio		Maximum possible accumulated agreement ratios remaining after this step	Maximum possible accumulated disagreement ratios, starting from the beginning
	Full agreement	Full disagreement		
1. SURNAME	2350/1	n/a	268 240 000 000/1	1/1
2. FIRST NAME	1260/1	1/39	212 880 000/1	1/39
3. SECOND NAME	1260/1	1/20	168 690/1	1/780
4. YEAR OF BIRTH	80/1	1/3	2 112/1	1/2 340
5. MONTH OF BIRTH	11/1	1/14	192/1	1/32 760
6. DAY OF BIRTH	24/1	1/6	8/1	1/196 560
7. PLACE OF BIRTH	8/1	1/18	1/1	1/3 538 080

designed to yield mainly global FREQUENCY RATIOS. These are later changed to their value-specific counterparts.

Two properties of the global frequencies of the comparison outcomes, and of their ratios, need to be kept in mind. The first is the absence of specificity for field value. The second is that the global frequency of a given outcome in the LINKED or in the UNLINKABLE pairs of records, encompasses or embraces the total definition of that comparison outcome, in other words including both the agreement and any non-agreement parts of the definition. When converting a global FREQUENCY RATIO to its value-specific counterpart, the first of these two properties is altered but not the second. This is the underlying concept.

The practical distinction, however, applies mainly to those identifiers that have many different values, such as the SURNAMES, INITIALS, GIVEN NAMES, and PLACES OF BIRTH. Only the *value non-specific* discriminating powers of these can conveniently be written into the comparison rules and accessed directly by the computer. The numerous *value-specific* discriminating powers have to be stored in sometimes lengthy look-up tables, and computer time is required to obtain the information. The refinement of doing the conversions and reassessing the discriminating powers is, for reasons of cost, applied only after the number of record pairs has been reduced as much as possible by the cruder but faster methods.

For other identifiers that have smaller numbers of different values, such as the various forms of MARITAL STATUS and the PLACES OF DEATH when broadly defined in relation to the PLACES OF WORK, the numbers of different outcome values will be smaller. It may then be convenient to recognize these possible values directly in the instructions to the computer. Thus, such comparisons may be made value specific from the beginning and no look-up tables need be employed. There is a double advantage wherever this is possible. It avoids the later 'conversion' step, and it is logically simpler and therefore less likely to go wrong.

In this latter situation, the FREQUENCY RATIOS possess the second of the two properties of the global variety (i.e. they reflect the full definition of the particular outcome), but not the first (i.e. they are not totally value non-specific). They are, as it were, already partially or wholly 'converted'.

Part IV

Organizing the product

28

Calculating absolute versus relative odds

The accumulated FREQUENCY RATIOS for a record pair represent only the 'RELATIVE' ODDS in favour of a correct match, not the 'ABSOLUTE' ODDS. They serve to array the matched pairs in order of the degree of assurance relative to one another, but they do not indicate what the actual 'betting odds' would be. It is quite possible, however, to do the conversion from RELATIVE ODDS to ABSOLUTE ODDS, and the latter are more useful than the former.

Where only the RELATIVE ODDS are calculated, assessment of the ABSOLUTE ODDS for a given pair requires visual scrutiny and subjective judgement. It was common practice at one time to search visually for the transition from predominantly 'good' links to predominantly 'bad', in a listing of matched pairs arrayed in descending order of assurance. A subjective 'threshold' was then set somewhere in the transition region, or perhaps two or more thresholds would be used to separate the 'good', the 'doubtful', and the 'bad' links.

A more objective method of assessing the ABSOLUTE ODDS, when it became available, was found to have distinct advantages. Subjective judgements were still made but they were made more quickly and easily. Moreover, small numbers of record pairs could now be seen to fall in unexpected places in the scale of assurances, and it was possible to investigate the reasons. For example, some pairs on which the name information agreed exceedingly well were seen to have strongly unfavourable ABSOLUTE ODDS. For these, the calculated ODDS could be shown to have been biased downwards by multiple correlated discrepancies of the date of birth components. The effect was seemingly due to 'multiple wrong guesses', perhaps made by informants who knew the names but not the DATES OF BIRTH. This sort of bias had not been anticipated.

The reason why the accumulated FREQUENCY RATIOS by themselves represent only the RELATIVE ODDS is that two factors influencing the ODDS are not taken into consideration: (1) the probability that a search record is indeed represented in the file being

searched, and (2) the size of that file. The less likely the search record
is to be there, and the larger that file, the greater will be the amount
of positive discriminating power required from the identifier comparisons to make a convincing case that a given record pair is a true
match. This may seem intuitively obvious, but the reasoning has
been debated in the past and is therefore discussed in greater detail in
Appendix B.

A simple procedure for converting RELATIVE ODDS to
ABSOLUTE ODDS, and a more refined alternative, are now
described.

28.1. A simple procedure

The most direct way of doing the conversion from the overall
RELATIVE ODDS to the ABSOLUTE ODDS, requires a preliminary
linkage. This is not especially inconvenient because calculation of
the FREQUENCY RATIOS likewise depends on data from a preliminary linkage.

The conversion formula for the absolute ODDS is as follows:

$$\text{ABSOLUTE ODDS} = \text{RELATIVE ODDS}$$
$$\times \frac{\text{number of linked search records}}{\text{total number of search records}}$$
$$\times \frac{1}{\text{total number of records being searched}}.$$

The first of the two fractions in the formula will only be known after
a trial linkage, but a small-scale manual search will usually be sufficient initially. Later, a more satisfactory value may be obtained from
the full-scale linkage, prior to the conversion of the FREQUENCY
RATIOS to their value-specific form. It is unlikely that this fraction
will change much with any further refinement of the linkage
product.

This simple approach has a fairly obvious consequence. Imagine a
file of 1000 work records being used to search a file of 1 000 000
death records, with 10 per cent of the workers being dead and therefore represented in the death file. For any particular work record,
the chance of finding a correct match by pure chance in a single try
will be $1/10 \times 1/1\,000\,000$, i.e., $1/10\,000\,000$. This is the initial
'hurdle' that the identifier agreements have to surmount in order to
make the odds 50:50 or better.

The overall RELATIVE ODDS are simply adjusted downwards by this factor (or 'hurdle') to convert them into ABSOLUTE ODDS.

28.2. Making the absolute odds 'age specific'

For the purpose of a death search, the simple procedure is crude in one respect; it fails to take into account the age of the individual. A young person is usually less likely to have died and be represented in a death file than is an older person. The bias from this source is less serious than one would imagine. But even so, an actuarial approach would represent a refinement and it is not too difficult to implement.

The reason that the bias from the simple approach is small is because really there are two biases and they operate in opposite directions. The opposing bias is from the FREQUENCY RATIOS for the year of birth differences, which are likewise not usually made age specific. Because the YEARS OF BIRTH for young people will be rare in the death file, agreement of them ought to carry greater *positive* discriminating power than would be the case for older people. This is what largely offsets the added *negative* discriminating power of the unlikelihood that a young person would be represented in the death file.

Because the balance is not precise, however, it would be best for both to be made age specific. The age would, of course, be computed differently in the two situations, and the adjustment would be carried out differently. The likelihood of having died would be based on the age when calculated by subtracting the year of birth as given on the search record, from the year of death as given on the death record. Life tables would then convert these ages to the required likelihoods of death. For the year of birth differences, the age would be based on the death record alone (usually by subtracting the year of birth from the year of death). The 'adjustment' of the FREQUENCY RATIOS for these would then be based on the 'rarity' or 'common-ness' of the particular age among the decedents. No prior linkages are required to make the approach work, and the details are rather straightforward.

The 'balance' referred to above may sometimes be far from precise. In the special case of cancer registry death clearance 'cancer life tables' are used to determine the likelihood of dying in a given year, and these may be based in part on the year of the diagnosis. But this does not alter the calculated age-specific likelihood of a year of birth agreement between a cancer record and a death record that are being compared with each other.

The implementation is greatly simplified if one thinks, conceptually, of searching just one year of deaths at a time. Whenever a search record is paired with a death record, one asks:

1. 'What is the chance that an individual of this age died in this one year?'
2. 'What is the size of the death file for this one year?'

The two questions are always specific for the calendar year of that particular death.

The likelihood that a person will die in a given year following his or her birth rises initially as he or she ages. Then it declines, starting somewhere around 80 years after birth in the case of males, because of the increasing likelihood that death has already occurred at an earlier age and the person is no longer 'available' to die later. This effect is seen in Table 28.1. The percentages in the final column of the Table are used as the age-specific likelihoods of dying in a single year. The file sizes that are used are the number of records in the death file pertaining to the particular year. For Canada, these have risen gradually over the years, the numbers for males being:

Table 28.1 Likelihoods of dying in given one-year periods after birth (males)

Years after birth	Still living (%)	Dying in year if alive (%)	Combined likelihood (dying in one year) (%)
20 (−4 to +5)	96.45	0.18	0.17
30 (−4 to +5)	94.85	0.15	0.14
40 (−4 to +5)	93.04	0.29	0.27
50 (−4 to +5)	88.82	0.76	0.68
60 (−4 to +5)	78.72	1.92	1.51
70 (−4 to +5)	58.58	4.44	2.60
80 (−4 to +5)	30.00	9.70	2.91
90 (−4 to +5)	6.49	20.98	1.36
100 (−4 and +)	0.19	41.97	0.08

1951	71 600 male deaths
1961	82 700
1971	91 800
1981	98 100

The above data may be employed without substantial error. However, they do not take account of the year in which a person was last known to be alive. There is an optional refinement that will adjust for this information. But the improvement is minor unless the person was quite old when 'last known to be alive'. In fact, until after age 70 the refinement will not make as much as a twofold difference. To apply the refinement, one simply divides by the percentage found in column 1 of Table 28.1, pertaining to the age at which the person was last known to have been alive. Knowledge that a person was recently still alive obviously raises the likelihood that he or she will have been 'available' to die in some subsequent year. The refinement is simple if one wishes to employ it.

A different approach is used to make the year of birth differences likewise age specific. The FREQUENCY RATIOS for these need to be adjusted upwards for the ages that are uncommon among the deaths, and downwards for those that are common. Table 28.2 indicates how this may be achieved. To make the FREQUENCY RATIOS

Table 28.2 Age-specific adjustment factors for year of birth differences (males)

Age-range	Deaths in the age-range as a fraction of all deaths (%)	Adjustment factor (= average % for all decades of life, divided by the % in this decade of life)
20 (−4 to +5)	1.55	9.7/1
30 (−4 to +5)	1.50	7.4/1
40 (−4 to +5)	2.68	4.2/1
50 (−4 to +5)	6.63	1.7/1
60 (−4 to +5)	14.72	1 /1.3
70 (−4 to +5)	25.26	1 /2.3
80 (−4 to +5)	28.46	1 /2.6
90 (−4 to +5)	11.63	1 /1.0
100 (−4 and +)	1.41	7.9/1

for the year of birth differences age specific, they are multiplied by the adjustment factors given in the final column of the Table.

The procedure outlined above, to make the ABSOLUTE ODDS age specific, is believed to be reasonably accurate. However, since there is no currently available alternative, it is sufficient for the result to be just 'empirically satisfactory'.

29

Setting an 'optimum' threshold

It is convenient to designate some level of OVERALL ODDS as a dividing line or 'threshold' separating the linkable from the unlinkable pairs of records. This is true even where later visual examination of borderline pairs leads one to relocate some of them from below the line upwards, and vice versa. Where the RELATIVE ODDS have been converted to ABSOLUTE ODDS, this threshold is unlikely to be far removed from the theoretical 50:50 odds point. Usually it is slightly above this point.

One should not assume that the 'best' threshold will necessarily be precisely at the 50:50 odds point. First, a different balance may be preferred, between the numbers of false links that get accepted versus the numbers of potential good links that get rejected; raising or lowering the threshold will alter the relative proportions of these two sorts of error. Second, there are biases in calculating a theoretical 50:50 odds point; correlated multiple discrepancies, for example, bias the calculated odds downwards; and the reverse is true of multiple agreements of identifiers that are not strictly independent of each other. And third, 50:50 odds are still not necessarily associated with 50 per cent of the records being 'good' links and 50 per cent being 'bad', even when allowance has been made for the known biases. This latter observation has not been fully explained.

The relationship between the calculated odds and the ratio of 'good' links to 'bad' has been found in practice to be especially unpredictable where the discriminating power of the identifiers is poor. For example, where the files contain many records with missing DATES OF BIRTH, the resulting lack of discriminating power usually serves to increase the numbers of record pairs with borderline overall odds. This excess often includes a high proportion of falsely matched pairs. As a result the threshold may have to be raised well above the theoretical 50:50 odds point in order to achieve a 50:50 ratio of false-positive to false-negative links.

A number of practical rules stem from these considerations:

1. The 50:50 A B S O L U T E O D D S point serves only as a rough guide to where an 'optimum' threshold is likely to be.
2. A conscious decision concerning the desired ratio of the two sorts of error is implied when choosing a threshold, and some alternative ratio may be preferred.
3. Estimates of the ratios of false-positive to false-negative links, based wholly on the theoretical odds, tend to differ from those derived empirically following manual resolutions of borderline links.
4. To minimize the problem of setting a threshold, it is best to exclude from a linkage operation those search records which lack adequate identifying particulars.

30

Grouping the matched pairs

Death searches are some of the simpler kinds of linkage because there is normally only one death record for an individual, and the files initiating the searches are usually purged of duplicate entries for any given person. As a result, the true links will almost always involve only one record from each of the two files.

The situation is less simple where either or both of the files may contain two or more records pertaining to the same person. The final product of a linkage operation should then be groups of records, with each group relating to a different individual. Where the personal identifiers are adequate, a linkage operation may still be fairly simple. However, where the discriminating powers are marginal, one will have to deal with multiple competing links. Such problems may be lessened by carrying out internal linkages within the two files. But where the internal linkages are borderline, the problems of grouping will remain.

The best tactic for dealing with the competing linkages to different groups seems to be to use a changing threshold. By setting the threshold high initially, the main groupings can be established with reasonable assurance. By thereafter lowering the threshold, one allows the records that make up these groups to compete for the hitherto unlinked records; in addition, new groups of a lower order of assurance get formed. There are few if any formal rules where final decisions have to be made concerning difficult groupings. For these, visual scrutiny and subjective judgement are required along with the calculated ABSOLUTE ODDS for the various links.

Considerable thought has been given at Statistics Canada to the problems of grouping, and to resolution of the associated conflicts. Moreover, their computer linkage system, known as GIRLS (Generalized Iterative Record Linkage System), has been designed to deal automatically with a substantial part of the problem and to permit manual intervention as well. (For more detail the reader is directed to the documentation of the GIRLS system by Hill and

Pring-Mill (1985, 1986), and in particular to the sections on 'Resolving conflicts within groups' contained in their 'Strategy guide' — see Bibliography.)

Most of the problems of linkage, and especially those associated with grouping, are caused by a deficiency of reliable personal identifying information on the records being linked. Where possible, much effort can be saved by excluding from a linkage operation those records for which this information falls below some predetermined minimum standard. For example, records that lack the full date of birth are obvious candidates for such exclusion. The final choice of a set of minimum standards is best based on experience. The objective is to limit the amount of clerical involvement in what should be a predominantly automated procedure.

Part V

Recapitulation and further thoughts

31

General summary and conclusions

The preceding chapters have attempted to outline in non-technical language the simple reasoning on which linkage is based. Two levels of sophistication have been described for applying this logic to decide whether a pair of records does, or does not, relate to the same person or family:

1. The use of *uncomplicated comparisons* of identifiers, so that even an inexperienced person may design reasonably efficient linkage procedures simply.
2. The use of *more thorough comparisons* that take note of almost any kind of clue that one would find helpful when doing the same job manually.

The first level of sophistication should obviously come before the second. But the second really does follow naturally enough if one is observant when examining difficult matches. It is by intimate contact with the records and the files that the art, as distinct from the science, of record linkage is developed. Insights come while doing the linkings. As we watch our own mind making a useful but less than simple comparison, we learn what comparison the computer could likewise usefully make. The machine can, and should, imitate the workings of the human mind, and it should do so in a highly flexible manner.

For the beginner, the most profitable exercise is to assemble by manual searching just a few hundred correctly matched pairs of records. Add to this a somewhat larger comparison file of randomly matched pairs, likewise manually assembled. Then, for any agreement, disagreement, or other comparison outcome, extract the frequency in the file of LINKED pairs and compare it with the frequency in the file of UNLINKABLE pairs. These FREQUENCY RATIOS, when applied to any matched pair of records and accumulated for that pair, will be seen to indicate whether the pair is correctly linked or not. Such hands-on work is a necessary complement to the related abstract thinking; without it, the understanding will remain incomplete and the application will suffer.

For the more experienced, those borderline links where one's subjective judgement conflicts with that of the computer should always be of special interest. These can properly become a continuing source of guidance and insight regarding the kinds of sophistication that would, and would not, be useful in the linkage procedure.

Finally, beware of rigid divisions of labour that create separate 'planners' and 'doers', because the 'doing' yields the feedback for the 'planning'. The best bridge between these functions is the mind of someone familiar with both.

32

Postscript

It is not for the uninitiated alone that plain language has been used in these discussions. A multiplicity of technical terms, despite their often laudable precision, can sometimes becloud simple thoughts. Experience has shown that even the older hands at the linkage business are not entirely immune from this source of confusion.

A case in point is the term 'WEIGHT'. I first used WEIGHTS that were logarithm to the base 2 in the late 1950s to make the FREQUENCY RATIOS addable. Being binary, they were called 'binit' WEIGHTS as in information theory. But I sometimes wonder if the use of the logarithms was a mistake. It simplified the calculations but complicated the thinking. Where the term 'WEIGHT' is applied to almost any logarithm regardless of its source, distinctions become blurred and origins forgotten. Moreover, they are so easily added and subtracted that the temptation is ever present to do this whether it is appropriate or not.

In the context of record linkage, the term 'WEIGHT' may refer to logarithms from at least three kinds of sources:

(1) a RATIO of two frequencies (i.e. of an *outcome* in linked versus unlinkable pairs);
(2) a frequency among *pairs* of records (i.e. of an *outcome* in LINKED or in UNLINKABLE pairs);
(3) a frequency among *unpaired* records (i.e. of a field *value* in a file).

The sources are the FREQUENCY RATIOS themselves, the NUMERATORS and the DENOMINATORS of these ratios, and various *substitutes* for and *estimates* of these numerators and denominators. The list could be extended to include WEIGHTS based on *adjustments* of various sorts. Rather than give such weights a variety of names in the present account, and thus create an unnecessary and confusing jargon, the sources themselves have been referred to directly by name instead, wherever possible.

In the past the WEIGHTS have, through oversight, been inappropriately added and subtracted in connection with the *early cut-off*, the *cross-comparisons*, and the *conversions* to value-specific ODDS. As well, there have been discussions about the propriety of adding the WEIGHTS for the outcomes from a series of related *conditional comparisons*. This is not necessarily wrong or necessarily right; it all depends on how the steps are arranged. The problem is that of designing a test to see whether it has been done correctly. An alternative that does not need to involve the summation of WEIGHTS uses a single comparison step with multiple alternative outcomes. This has a built-in check; if the outcome frequencies do not add up to 100 per cent, a mistake has been made. This check has no simple analogue using WEIGHTS.

The non-technical language of the present account is not just an attempt to bridge a gap between specialties. The intention is broader; it is to bypass the formalizations wherever they threaten to supplant the intuitive understanding of a simple concept.

Appendices and bibliography

Appendix A:

Definitions

Most words have been used here in their common-sense capacities only, but just a few have narrower connotations as applied to record linkage. It may help to explain the more specific of these usages.

BLOCKING. The use of sequencing information (e.g. the phonetically coded versions of the surnames) to divide the files into '*pockets*'. Normally, records are only compared with each other where they are from the same 'pocket', i.e. have identical blocking information. The purpose is to avoid having to compare the enormous numbers of record pairs that would be generated if every record in the file initiating the searches were allowed to pair with every record in the file being searched.

DENOMINATOR. This usually refers to the denominator in a FREQUENCY RATIO, i.e. the frequency of a given comparison outcome among UNLINKABLE pairs of records brought together at random. It may be applied also to one of the two components of any ODDS.

FREQUENCY RATIO. The frequency of a given comparison outcome among correctly LINKED pairs of records, divided by the corresponding frequency among UNLINKABLE pairs brought together at random. The comparison outcome may be defined in any way, for example as a full agreement, a partial agreement, a more extreme disagreement, or any combination of values from the two records that are being compared. The FREQUENCY RATIO may be specific for the particular value of an identifier when it agrees, or for the value of the agreement portion of an identifier that partially agrees, or it may be non-specific for value.

GENERAL FREQUENCY. A weighted mean of the frequencies of the various values of an identifier among the individual (i.e. *unpaired*) records of the file being searched. It is non-specific for value. Value-specific frequencies are also obtained from the same source.

GLOBAL FREQUENCY. The frequency of a comparison outcome among *pairs* of records, when that outcome is defined in terms that are non-specific for the value of the identifier. The outcome may be a full agreement, a partial agreement, or a more extreme disagreement. The record pairs may be those of a LINKED file, or they may be UNLINKABLE pairs brought together at random. Only in the special case of the full agreement outcomes are the global and the general frequencies numerically equal, but they always remain conceptually different. The difference is that a global frequency, although value non-specific, always reflects the *full definition* of the particular outcome, including both the agreement portion and the non-agreement portion of that definition. A general frequency cannot do this because it is based on a file of single (i.e. *unpaired*) records.

GLOBAL FREQUENCY RATIO. The ratio of the global frequency for a particular comparison outcome among LINKED pairs of records, divided by the corresponding frequency among UNLINKABLE pairs. It is equivalent to the global ODDS. GLOBAL FREQUENCY RATIOS for agreement outcomes and partial agreement outcomes are often subsequently converted to their value-specific counterparts during the linkage process. The conversion is accomplished by means of an adjustment upwards where the agreement portion of the identifier has a rare value, and an adjustment downwards where the value is common.

LINKAGE. In its broadest sense, RECORD LINKAGE is the bringing together of information from two or more records that are believed to relate to the same 'entity'. For an economic or social study, the 'entities' in question might be farms or businesses. For a health study, the 'entities' of special interest are usually individual people or families. It is in the latter sense that the word is used throughout this book.

LINKED In line with the above definition of 'record linkage', LINKED pairs of records are pairs believed to relate to the same individual or family (or other kind of entity). Record pairs brought together and judged *not* to relate to the same individual or family may be referred to as 'UNLINKABLE' pairs. For short, the two sorts of pairs are sometimes called 'LINKS' and 'NON-LINKS' respectively. As used here, the term implies that some sort of decision has been reached concerning the likely correctness of the *match*.

MATCHED. This word is variously used in the literature on record linkage. In this book, however, it is given no special technical meaning and merely implies a pairing of records on the basis of some stated similarity (or dissimilarity). For example, early in a linkage operation, records from the two files being LINKED are normally *matched* for agreement of the surname code. The resulting pairs may also be called '*candidate pairs*' for linkage, but this emphasis is most appropriate in the later stages when the numbers of competing pairs have diminished. Pairs of records will frequently be spoken of as 'correctly *matched*', 'falsely *matched*', or 'randomly *matched*'.

NUMERATOR. This usually refers to the numerator in a FREQUENCY RATIO, i.e. the frequency of a given comparison outcome among pairs of records believed to be correctly LINKED. It may be applied also to one of the two components of any ODDS.

ODDS. This word is used in its ordinary sense but is applied in a number of situations. As relating to a particular outcome from the comparison of a given identifier it is synonymous with the FREQUENCY RATIO for that outcome. As relating to the accumulated FREQUENCY RATIOS for a given record pair it refers to the overall RELATIVE ODDS. It is also applied to the overall ABSOLUTE ODDS.

OUTCOME. This refers to any *outcome* or result from the comparison of a particular identifier (or concatenated identifiers) on a pair of records, or the comparison of a particular identifier on one record with a different but logically related identifier on the other. It may be defined in almost any way, for example as an AGREEMENT, a PARTIAL AGREEMENT, a more *extreme* DISAGREEMENT, any other SIMILARITY or DISSIMILARITY, or the *absence* of an identifier on one record as compared with its presence or absence on the other. An outcome may be specific for a particular value of an identifier (e.g. as it appears on the search record) or for any part of that identifier, especially where there is an agreement or partial agreement; it may be non-specific for value; or it may even be specific for a particular kind of DISAGREEMENT defined in terms of any pair of values being compared.

VALUE. An identifier (e.g. an initial) may be said to have a number of different 'values' (e.g. initial 'A', initial 'B', and so on). Surnames, given names, and places of birth have many possible values. Other identifiers tend to have fewer values that need to be distinguished from each other.

WEIGHT. In the literature, this term has been widely applied to the logarithms of various entities, such as:

(1) a FREQUENCY RATIO for a specified outcome from the comparison of a given identifier;
(2) the product of all the FREQUENCY RATIOS for a given record pair;
(3) the NUMERATOR of a particular FREQUENCY RATIO;
(4) the DENOMINATOR of a particular FREQUENCY RATIO;
(5) any *estimate* of such a numerator or denominator, not obtained directly from a file of matched pairs of records.

The use of the logarithm is merely a convenience when doing the arithmetic; it does not affect the logic except to make it appear more complicated. The term 'WEIGHT' has therefore been employed sparingly in this book. Instead, reference has been made directly to the source frequency or FREQUENCY RATIO, or to the *estimates* of these, wherever possible.

Appendix B:

Derivations

There was considerable discussion at one time concerning the calculation of ABSOLUTE ODDS for the linkages from a death search, using the likelihood of death in a given period and the size of the death file covering that period.

The general formula for ABSOLUTE ODDS is as follows:

$$\text{ABSOLUTE ODDS} = \text{RELATIVE ODDS} \times \frac{\text{number of linked pairs}}{\text{all possible matched pairs of records}}.$$

where 'all possible matched pairs' is equal to the product of the numbers of records in the two files being linked (i.e. all pairs that would be formed if every record in the file initiating the searches were compared with every record in the file being searched).

The final term of the above formula breaks down into two terms:

$$\frac{\text{linked search records}}{\text{all search records}} \times \frac{1}{\text{all records being searched}}.$$

This is the form in which the general formula is correctly applied to convert RELATIVE ODDS into ABSOLUTE ODDS. For a death search, the first of these two terms is equal to the probability that a search record will be represented in the death file covering the specified period.

Note: The term in the first formula that has been expanded in this manner is sometimes *wrongly* written as a ratio instead of a proportion, in other words as

$$\frac{\text{number of linked pairs}}{\text{all possible non-linked pairs}}.$$

This ratio may be shown by means of an extreme example to yield a false answer. Imagine a search file of just one record, and a death file being searched that likewise consists of just a single record, to which the search record is correctly linkable. Now, when the cohort represented by the search file is followed to extinction and there are no non-linked search records, the expression becomes equal to infinity, whereas its correct value should be unity.

Moreover, if both of the two component terms are expressed as ratios, they will equal infinity for a cohort that is followed to extinction, regardless of the sizes of the cohort and the death file. The true value, or course, should be unity.

Appendix C:

Typical identifier frequencies

For purposes of planning, it is sometimes useful to know the typical frequencies of selected values of the more important identifiers. This is especially true of the SURNAMES, and of the male and female GIVEN NAMES. For each of these we give here:

(1) the *specific* frequencies of the more common values of the names; and
(2) the *general* frequencies for both the full alphabetical versions, and the truncated versions of these names.

The frequencies are derived from the Canadian Mortality Data Base at Statistics Canada, and the data are those of Pierre Lalonde of the Occupational and Environmental Health Research Unit, Vital Statistics and Health Status Section, Health Division, Statistics Canada.

Surnames

1. The 20 most common surnames with their frequencies

Rank	Surname (7 characters)	Frequency (%)	Rank	Surname (7 characters)	Frequency (%)
1	SMITH	0.720	11	ROY	0.243
2	BROWN	0.389	12	JONES	0.230
3	WILSON	0.316	13	THOMPSO	0.229
4	MACDONA	0.303	14	MILLER	0.226
5	JOHNSON	0.285	15	GAGNON	0.211
6	MARTIN	0.285	16	WILLIAM	0.206
7	TREMBLA	0.276	17	WHITE	0.200
8	ANDERSO	0.265	18	JOHNSTO	0.196
9	CAMPBEL	0.264	19	LEBLANC	0.190
10	TAYLOR	0.254	20	YOUNG	0.190

2. General frequencies of surname NYSIIS codes plus different
numbers of characters of the alphabetical surnames

Code + characters	General frequency (per 10 000)
NYSIIS(6) + SURNAME(7)	4.379
NYSIIS(6) + SURNAME(4)	4.864
NYSIIS(6) codes alone	8.714

Male given names

1. The 20 most common male given names with their frequencies

Rank	Given name (7 characters)	Frequency (%)	Rank	Given name (7 characters)	Frequency (%)
1	JOHN	5.304	11	ARTHUR	1.477
2	WILLIAM	4.829	12	ALBERT	1.348
3	JAMES	3.155	13	ALEXAND	1.085
4	JOSEPH	2.964	14	FREDERI	1.043
5	GEORGE	2.613	15	DAVID	0.949
6	CHARLES	1.982	16	ERNEST	0.907
7	ROBERT	1.884	17	ALFRED	0.874
8	THOMAS	1.816	18	FRANK	0.831
9	HENRY	1.605	19	PAUL	0.762
10	EDWARD	1.590	20	PETER	0.761

2. General frequencies of male given names with various degrees of
truncation

Degree of truncation (characters remaining)	General frequency (per 10 000)
First 7 characters	114.595
First 4 characters	128.748
First 3 characters	146.878
First 2 characters	263.486
First 1 character (initial)	729.868

Female given names

1. The 20 most common female GIVEN NAMES with their frequencies

Rank	Given name (7 characters)	Frequency (%)	Rank	Given name (7 characters)	Frequency (%)
1	MARY	3.438	11	ANNA	1.156
2	ELIZABE	2.922	12	ROSE	1.102
3	MARGARE	2.476	13	FLORENC	1.077
4	MARIE	1.764	14	SARAH	1.029
5	JANE	1.621	15	ANNE	0.996
6	ANNIE	1.593	16	CATHERI	0.929
7	ANN	1.542	17	ELLEN	0.917
8	MAY	1.463	18	AGNES	0.883
9	ALICE	1.419	19	EDITH	0.855
10	LOUISE	1.170	20	HELEN	0.835

2. General frequencies of female given names with various degrees of truncation

Degree of truncation (characters remaining)	General frequency (per 10 000)
First 7 characters	66.718
First 4 characters	86.660
First 3 characters	195.751
First 2 characters	368.795
First 1 character (initial)	985.084

Appendix D:

Linking special disease registers

Health follow-up studies frequently make use of registers of special diseases such as cancers and congenital anomalies, both as starting-point and as end-point files. Moreover, the registries themselves may wish to do internal linkages and death searches for their own purposes. The matching procedures for such special applications can differ in two important respects from those commonly employed in following up a normally healthy cohort.

First, the diagnoses may usefully be regarded as yet a further kind of personal identifying information, agreement or similarity of which will contribute to the calculated overall odds in favour of a correct link. Rare diagnoses will carry greater discriminating power when they agree than will the more common diagnoses, and this is true whether one is doing an internal linkage to purge a file of duplicate entries, or is carrying out a death search.

Second, for the purposes of a death search the registrants cannot be viewed as having the same life expectancies as members of the general population. The disease must be taken into account when calculating the likelihood that an individual could have died in a given year and therefore be represented in the death file for that year. Life tables for such persons are best based on the particular diagnosis as well as on age and sex. For cancer cases in particular, the number of years that have elapsed since the diagnosis was made will often be as important in influencing the risk of death as is the diagnosis itself. In principle, there is no obstacle to compiling the appropriate tables of survival and death rates, where these are known, but the computer would have to access a considerably larger set of look-up tables than when doing a corresponding death search for a normally healthy cohort.

Appropriate double use of the diagnostic information is implied for the death searches, just as with the age/date of birth information for a 'normal' cohort. 'Normally', *age* is taken to affect the 'propen-

sity' for being represented in the death file; and *calendar* Y E A R O F
B I R T H, which is correlated with age, can affect the D I S-
C R I M I N A T I N G P O W E R of an agreement or partial agreement of
that year. With the 'normal' cohort these two effects will tend to
cancel out partially. For example, because a normal young person is
relatively unlikely to die in a given 12-month period, this should
argue *against* a correct match with a death record for a year in which
he or she is still young. Over against this, agreement or partial agreement of the person's year of birth with that given on such a death
record should argue more strongly *in favour of* a correct match,
purely because it is a rare year of birth for the decedents in that year
of deaths. This kind of partial balance, between the two opposing
effects of the age specificity, largely disappears when the person in
question is already known to have a less-than-average life
expectancy. Thus, the refinement provided by the double use of the
age/year of birth specificity, and by any other indicators of the 'propensity' for being in the death file, such as the diagnosis, acquires
added importance wherever death searches are initiated by records
from a register of special diseases.

For precision in any death search, it is prudent to take into account
as many as possible of the specificities that influence both

(1) the probability of fortuitous agreement of any identifier (e.g. year of
birth, or diagnosis) that is known to be correlated with the likelihood of
death; and
(2) the effect of that identifier on the probability of being represented in the
death file that is searched (conceptually, the file for just the single year
of deaths represented by the particular death record being compared).

Where it is a work record that initiates a death search, we may
reasonably regard the individual as more or less 'normal'. The likelihoods of death and of chance agreement of the year of birth are then
only required to be specific for age and sex. But the relevant specificities increase in number once we know the individual is sick and
has a diagnosis. Age may then become the least important of these
specificities.

For those enrolled in a special disease register, the important
specificities (other than sex) are likely to be concerned with the
diagnosis, the *years since the diagnosis*, and the *age* at the time of
the diagnosis, probably in that order. All of these will affect the
'propensity' for being represented in the death file; and the diagnosis
becomes a personal identifier as well.

The conversion formula for deriving ABSOLUTE ODDS from RELATIVE ODDS remains the same as before, except that a probability is substituted for a frequency. Thus, the middle term of the expression,

$$
\begin{aligned}
\text{ABSOLUTE ODDS} \;=\; &\text{RELATIVE ODDS} \\
&\times \frac{\text{number of linked search records}}{\text{total number of search records}} \\
&\times \frac{1}{\text{total number of records being searched}}
\end{aligned}
$$

becomes simply the '*probability that the particular search record is potentially linkable*'. Recognition of multiple specificities does require that more look-up tables be used when estimating the probability that a particular search record is represented in a death file. But the handling of the variables is not especially complicated.

In the sections that follow we consider, (1) the use of diagnosis as a personal identifier, and (2) diagnosis as affecting the likelihood of death in a given year.

D.1. Diagnosis as a personal identifier

Diagnosis may be treated as a personal identifier that will help to establish a correct link. An early indication of its likely usefulness may be gained by carrying out a few linkages manually before attempting to design a comparison procedure. It should be equally helpful for internal linkages and for death searches.

The examples considered here relate mainly to death searches initiated by cancer records, but the comparison steps are similar for other kinds of diseases and other kinds of linkage. As with names and initials, the first comparison step and the FREQUENCY RATIOS it yields are usually non-specific for value. The specificities are taken into account in a second step when specific ADJUSTMENT FACTORS are used to convert the global FREQUENCY RATIOS to their value-specific counterparts.

The diagnosis on a cancer record will frequently occupy two fields, one for the designations 'malignant' versus 'benign', and the other for the detailed diagnosis as an international code number. The comparisons of these two components might be handled

Table D.1 Global frequency ratios for different levels of agreement of cancer diagnoses in death searches initiated by records of malignancies (male) (cancer 'site' is defined by three digits of the International Code)

Outcome (cancer record vs. matching death record)	Percentage frequencies		Frequency ratios (links/ non-links)
	Links	Non-links	
Cancer–cancer, site agrees	45.3	2.6	17.4/1
Cancer–cancer, site disagrees	17.1	16.8	1.0/1
Cancer–other	37.6	80.6	1 /2.1
Other–cancer			n/a
Other–other			n/a

separately, but the logic and the mechanics are simpler if they are concatenated and a single comparison procedure is employed which yields multiple outcome levels. An example is given in Table D.1.

When the specific cancer diagnosis or site is later taken into consideration, those that are rare should produce higher-than-average FREQUENCY RATIOS when they agree, and those that are common should yield lower-than-average FREQUENCY RATIOS. The appropriate ADJUSTMENT FACTORS are calculated as described earlier for names and initials. Examples are given in Table D.2.

There is nothing special about the manner in which the diagnosis is treated when using it as an item of personal identification. It may be employed much like a name, or an initial, or a place of birth.

D.2. Diagnosis as affecting the likelihood of death in the years that follow

Diagnosis can serve a quite different purpose in a linkage operation, especially where the objective is a death search. Different diagnoses influence to different degrees the 'propensity' for an individual to be represented in a relevant death file. The effect of this 'propensity' on the calculated overall odds in favour of a correct match may be calculated. Where an ongoing series of death searches is

Table D.2 Specific adjustment factors for agreements of cancer
site — 10 most common sites (male)

Cancer site	General frequency (%)	Specific frequency (%)*	Adjustment factor (general/specific frequency)
1. Lung, trachea, bronchus	13.2	31.3	1/2.4
2. Prostate	13.2	9.5	1.4/1
3. Colon	13.2	7.8	1.7/1
4. Stomach	13.2	7.3	1.8/1
5. Pancreas	13.2	5.7	2.3/1
6. Rectum, anus, sigmoid junction	13.2	3.8	3.5/1
7. Bladder	13.2	3.1	4.3/1
8. Brain	13.2	2.5	5.3/1
9. Kidney, other urinary	13.2	2.3	5.7/1
10. Oesophagus	13.2	2.2	6.0/1
Other	13.2	<2.2	>6.0/1

*Percentage frequency among cancer deaths.

contemplated, the added precision will be well worth the effort of
setting up the diagnosis-related data. We consider especially the
death searches initiated by cancer records.

The likelihood that a given individual is represented in a particular
death file is most readily calculated if one thinks, conceptually, of
searching just one year of deaths at a time. Even though the actual
search involves many years of death records that are interfiled with
each other, one may still ask for a given matched pair of records:

1. What is the likelihood that this cancer registrant is represented in this
   particular year of deaths?
2. How large is the death file for that year?

These two kinds of information are required by the formula which
derives ABSOLUTE ODDS from overall RELATIVE ODDS. In
practice, it is best to employ separate files for the two sexes, and to
treat the above questions as relating to just one sex or the other.

The data for the calculation would be broken down by the

diagnosis, the number of *years since the diagnosis* was made, and the *age-group* at the time of the diagnosis. This breakdown creates a separate two-dimensional matrix for each diagnosis, within the particular sex. Each cell of a given matrix contains the likelihood that an individual of that description will die in the particular 12-month period. This is the product of the likelihood that the individual is still alive at the beginning of the period, and therefore 'available' to die, *times* the likelihood of dying in the next 12 months if he or she has survived that long.

The construction of such matrices is not a difficult task provided the data are available. Once constructed, they could be used repeatedly. Separate matrices would obviously be required for the 10 most common causes of cancer deaths for each of the two sexes, and these together would cover between 70 and 75 per cent of all cancer deaths. Separate matrices would also be required for a few of the other major categories of malignancy, but rarer diagnoses could be judiciously grouped for convenience. Such tables may sometimes be prepared from the data accumulated in a well-organized cancer register.

The use of the matrices is simple. To illustrate this we consider the examples of two cancer records containing quite different diagnoses. The first is the record of a male with lung cancer. The second is that of a female with breast cancer. The relevant data are given in Tables D.3 and D.4 respectively. Large differences will be noted in the annual death rates for the two conditions.

In the first example of the *male* with *lung cancer*, let us suppose that he was in the age-range 74 + when the diagnosis was made, and that his cancer record is being compared with the record of a death that occurred 5 years after his diagnosis. The probability that he died in that particular year is given in Table D.3, in the cell defined by the last of the three columns pertaining to his age-group, and by the line for the 12-month period starting 5 years after the diagnosis. The relevant probability is 0.7 per cent. This is simply incorporated into the formula for deriving ABSOLUTE ODDS from the corresponding overall RELATIVE ODDS. With Canadian deaths, the size of a death file for males dying in a single year would vary from 82 000 for the period 1950–65, to 99 500 for the period starting in 1975. These two pieces of information are all that are needed. One might perhaps want to employ even finer breakdowns by diagnosis and age-group; if so, the number of look-up tables would be increased, but the

Table D.3 Survival and risk of death by years following diagnosis — lung cancer (male)

Start of the yearly interval after diagnosis	Age 0–74 years (88%)			Age 75 + years (12%)		
	% still living at the start of the year	% of survivors dying in the year	% of cohort dying within the year	% still living at the start of the year	% of survivors dying in the year	% of cohort dying within the year
At diagnosis	100.0	65.4	65.4	100.0	76.7	76.7
1 year	34.6	43.6	15.1	23.3	48.9	11.4
2 years	19.5	23.6	4.6	11.9	37.0	4.4
3 years	14.9	12.1	1.8	7.5	32.0	2.4
4 years	13.1	9.2	1.2	5.1	23.5	1.2
5 years	11.9	8.4	1.0	3.9	17.9	0.7
6 years	10.9	8.3	0.9	3.2	15.6	0.5
7 years	10.0	8.0	0.8	2.7	11.1	0.3
8 years	9.2	7.6	0.7	2.4	8.3	0.2
9 years	8.5	3.5	0.3	2.2	4.5	0.1
10 years	8.2	—	—	2.2	—	—

Median survival time: age 0–74 = 0.8 years; age 75 + = 0.7 years.

mechanics of preparing and using them would remain the same.

In the second example of the *female* with *breast cancer*, let us suppose that she was in the age-range 0–74 years when the diagnosis was made, and that her cancer record is being compared with the record of a death that occurred 8 years after her diagnosis. The probability that she died in that particular year will be seen from Table D.4 to be 2.4 per cent. The number of female deaths in a single year, in Canada, varied from 58 000 to 70 500 for the periods mentioned above. As with the example shown in Table D.3, these two pieces of information are simply 'plugged into' the formula for deriving ABSOLUTE ODDS from the corresponding overall RELATIVE ODDS.

Having described a refined procedure, let us now consider what cruder alternatives exist, and whether there are any useful short cuts for obtaining the benefits of diagnostic specificity with less work.

Table D.4 Survival and risk of death by years following diagnosis — breast cancer (female)

Start yearly of the yearly internal after diagnosis	Age 0–74 years (88%)			Age 75 + years (12%)		
	% still living at the start of the year	% of survivors dying in the year	% of cohort dying within the year	% still living at the start of the year	% of survivors dying in the year	% of cohort dying within the year
At diagnosis	100.0	5.9	5.9	100.0	15.2	15.2
1 year	94.1	7.7	7.2	84.8	14.6	12.4
2 years	86.9	7.6	6.6	72.4	14.2	10.3
3 years	80.3	6.5	5.2	62.1	13.5	8.4
4 years	75.1	5.9	4.4	53.7	13.2	7.1
5 years	70.7	5.1	3.6	46.6	13.0	6.1
6 years	67.1	4.8	3.2	40.5	12.5	5.1
7 years	63.9	4.4	2.8	35.4	11.6	4.1
8 years	61.1	3.9	2.4	31.3	10.2	3.2
9 years	58.7	3.6	2.1	28.1	9.6	2.7
10 years	56.6	—	—	25.4	—	—

Median survival time: age 0–74 = 10 + years; age 75 + = 4.5 years.

The crudest approach is to ignore the cancer site entirely. Then, if one thinks in terms of searching the whole of a national death file, the *average* likelihood that a registrant will be represented there will be essentially the same as the proportion of registrants known to be dead. Most registries do a clerical follow-up, so this proportion is usually known in advance. (The computerized death search will in such circumstances serve as a check on the adequacy of the clerical death searches.) If, for example, some 60 per cent of the registered male cases of malignancy are believed to be dead, that will be the figure to use in the formula as the 'likelihood of being represented in the file being searched'. With this approach, the 'size of the file being searched', called for in the formula, will be the size of the death file for all years combined.

A slightly less crude approach likewise ignores the cancer site, but treats the search, conceptually, as being carried out in one year of death records at a time. Sometimes like 8 per cent of the registrants known to be alive at the beginning of a year will die during the year. That figure may be used for death searches initiated by registrants who are not known to be dead. With this approach, the 'size of the file being searched', called for in the formula, will be the size of the death file for just a single year.

Various ways have been tried of using the specificities of the cancer sites in this connection without going to the lengths of constructing site-specific life tables as shown above. Earlier versions of this approach proved cumbersome, but a simplified version may now be recommended. This is now described in Section D.3.

D.3. Simplifying the calculation of the 'propensity' for dying in a given year after diagnosis

There is need for a simplified procedure with which to estimate the likelihood of dying in a given year after a diagnosis of cancer (or of any other condition recognized by a special disease register). This need arises when doing death searches, because of:

(1) the collective size of the life tables when prepared separately for the various age-groups and diagnoses; and

(2) the frequent chance statistical fluctuations for the individual years following diagnosis, especially where the condition is rare and the data are thinly spread over the cells of a breakdown.

Despite the limited success of earlier attempts at simplification, there is now a workable procedure that is reasonably accurate.

The survival patterns following the various diagnoses differ from each other in two important respects. First, the long-term (e.g. 10-year) survivals vary widely with the diagnoses. Second, the proportions of earlier versus later deaths (e.g. within the 10-year period) also differ, independently from the long-term survival. These two characteristics may be quantified separately. The method described here makes use of the 10-year survival rates for cancers originating in the various body sites. It also distinguishes between those kinds of cancer for which the annual risk of death among survivors is relatively constant over the years following the diagnosis, versus those for which the risk declines among the cases who have survived the earlier years.

These long-term survivals can usually be fairly accurately determined, even where the data are too few to yield reliable risks of death for each of the post-diagnosis years. Moreover, one would not be wildly wrong if one were to assume, as an approximation, that the annual risk of death among survivors remained constant from the time of the diagnosis over as much as 10 years. Only occasionally will this approximation underestimate the numbers of deaths in the first year by much more than threefold, or overestimate those in the 10th year by a similar factor.

This partial solution is recommended, therefore, to those who want maximum simplicity. As a rough rule of thumb, it is unwise to casually ignore differences in discriminating power that will alter the overall ABSOLUTE ODDS by much in excess of twofold. The patently false assumption of a constant annual risk of death among the survivors does lead to errors in the vicinity of threefold, and so is borderline with respect to this rule. However, acceptance of the simplifying assumption is preferable to the cruder alternatives mentioned in Section D.2.

Those who wish to use this partial solution, for example for cancer registry death searches, will find that the treatment of the actual data is simple enough. Only the 10-year survivals for the various cancer diagnoses, broken down by the different age-groups at diagnosis, are required as input. The average annual survival rates among those cases who have lived to the beginning of a given year in the 10-year period will be the 1/10th power of this, and the average annual death rates will be 'one minus the corresponding survival rates'. The necessary calculations may be performed rapidly on any scientific pocket calculator with a function key for 'y^x'. Table D.5 shows the resulting estimated numbers of cases in a cohort of 1000, that would be expected to die over the 10 successive 12-month periods following the diagnosis, given various 10-year survival rates. The Table may be used directly, or a finer breakdown may be calculated with little effort.

For those who want a more precise solution that is still simple, information is needed on the degrees to which this treatment underestimates the numbers of deaths in the earlier years after diagnosis, and overestimates those in the later years. It is convenient here to divide the more common cancers into three categories which we will call groups I, II, and III. Within these groups, the 'observed/expected' deaths in the initial year after diagnosis will approximate 1, 2, and 3 respectively. (In the final year of the 10-year

Table D.5 Expected deaths in successive 1-year periods following diagnosis, assuming a constant death rate among survivors

10-year survival per 1000 diagnosed*	Average annual death rate per 1000 survivors**	Expected deaths by successive 12-month intervals following diagnosis† (per 1000 at time of diagnosis)					
		1st	2nd	3rd	4th	5th	6–10th (average)
10	369	369	233	147	93	58	18
20	324	324	219	148	100	68	25
50	259	259	192	142	105	78	35
100	206	206	163	130	103	82	43
150	173	173	143	118	98	81	47
200	149	149	127	108	92	78	49
300	105	105	94	84	75	67	48
400	88	88	80	73	67	61	46
500	67	67	62	58	54	51	41
600	50	50	47	45	43	41	35
700	35	35	34	33	31	30	27
800	22	22	22	22	21	21	19

* The *10-year survival* ('x') is the proportion of the original cases surviving 10 years after diagnosis. It is expressed here as the number remaining from 1000 cases living at the time of diagnosis.

**The *average annual death rate* ('d') is the annual rate which, if constant over the 10 12-month intervals following diagnosis, would result in the given 10-year survival. It is expressed here as the number of cases dying in any 12-month interval among 1000 survivors alive at the beginning of that interval. The proportion of these survivors dying in the succeeding 12 months ('d') is given by the expression

$$d = (1 - p) = [1 - (x^{1/10})]$$

where 'p' is the proportion surviving the 1-year period.

†The *expected deaths* ('d_n') in a particular one of the 12-month intervals following diagnosis are expressed here as per 1000 cases alive at the time of diagnosis. The proportion of this original cohort dying in the 'n'th interval is given by the expression

$$d_n = p^{n-1} \cdot d.$$

period, the corresponding factors will be approximately 1/1, 1/2, and 1/3.)

These factors may be treated as ADJUSTMENT FACTORS when using the formula to convert from overall RELATIVE ODDS to ABSOLUTE ODDS. They are largely independent of the long-term survival rates, and independent also from the derived estimates of the likelihoods of death in the individual years following diagnosis. Actual observed/expected ratios are given in Tables D.6, D.7 and D.8 for the three groups of cancer diagnoses. It is suggested that the averages at the bottoms of these Tables, for the ratios of observed/expected, be used instead of the values contained in the individual lines of the Tables. The Tables are based on unpublished data for the Alberta Cancer Registry, provided by Mr Ron Dewar and Dr G. B. Hill in 1982.

Tables D.5–D.8 deserve comment. The arrangement of the different cancers groups I, II, and III reflects the degree of heterogeneity of the cancers affecting a given organ site. Where the cancers at that site all have similar survival characteristics, there will be a relatively constant annual death rate among the survivors, such as is observed with breast cancer and prostate cancer. Where cancers that are dissimilar in this respect affect the same organ, those that kill early will tend to disappear over time leaving cases of the less virulent forms still alive, as with the various cancers of the lung. This is really a truism, but the present groupings do help to create a quantitative as well as a qualitative distinction. Moreover, the distinction holds relatively constant for a given cancer site, despite the variations in long-term survival associated with differences in sex and in age-group at the time of diagnosis. Finally, the 'number of cases at outset' given in the Tables should not be regarded as representing a continuously followed cohort. By the nature of a provincial registry, cases do leave the cohort by migrating out of the province, and others may enter it by the reverse process.

If Tables D.5–D.8 are used in an actual death search, consideration must be given to the diagnoses that they do not cover. The Tables refer to only 21 cancer sites, i.e. those most commonly affected, whereas the three-digit codings of the International Classification recognize a total of 62. Corresponding data for the less frequent diagnoses are not as clear cut as those shown here. Unless the user wishes to continue the data extraction described above, using a much larger cancer file, the simplest alternative will be to

Table D.6 Observed versus 'expected' deaths in successive 1-year periods following diagnosis — group I cancer sites ('expected' deaths are calculated on an annual death rate for survivors that is constant over successive yearly intervals following diagnosis)

10-year survival per 1000 diagnosed*	Average annual death rate per 1000 survivors	Observed/expected deaths in the 12-month intervals following diagnosis						Sex and age at diagnosis	Cancer site	No. of cases at outset
		1st	2nd	3rd	4th	5th	6–10th (average)			
153	171	1.3	1.1	1.2	1.1	0.9	0.7	M 75+	Prostate	(2620)
298	114	0.9	1.1	1.1	1.1	0.9	0.9	M 0–74	Prostate	(3382)
254	128	1.2	1.1	1.1	1.0	1.0	0.9	F 75+	Breast	(1242)
566	55	1.0	1.4	1.4	1.1	1.1	0.8	F 0–74	Breast	(9316)
329	105	0.8	1.0	1.1	1.1	1.1	1.0	M 75+	Lip	(401)
773	25	0.7	1.0	1.2	1.0	1.2	1.0	M 0–75	Lip	(1837)
412	85	0.9	1.1	1.0	1.2	1.0	1.0	M 75+	Skin	(3658)
524	63	0.8	1.0	0.9	0.9	0.8	0.9	F 75+	Skin	(2143)
803	13	1.2	1.0	0.9	1.0	1.1	1.1	M 0–74	Skin	(8465)
896	11	0.6	1.0	0.9	1.3	1.0	1.0	F 0–74	Skin	(6137)
Average		0.9	1.1	1.1	1.1	1.0	0.9			

* The *10-year survival* ('x') is the proportion of the original cases surviving 10 years after diagnosis. It is expressed here as the number remaining from 1000 cases living at the time of diagnosis.

**The *average annual death rate* ('d') is the annual rate which, if constant over the 10 12-month intervals following diagnosis, would result in the given 10-year survival. It is expressed here as the number of cases dying in any 12-month interval among 1000 survivors alive at the beginning of that interval. The proportion of these survivors dying in the succeeding 12 months ('d') is given by the expression

$$d = (1 - p) = [1 - (x^{1/10})]$$

where 'p' is the proportion surviving the 1-year period.

†The *expected deaths* ('d_n') in a particular one of the 12-month intervals following diagnosis are expressed here as per 1000 cases alive at the time of diagnosis. The proportion of this original cohort dying in the 'n'th interval is given by the expression

$$d_n = p^{n-1} \cdot d.$$

Table D.7 Observed versus 'expected' deaths in successive 1-year periods following diagnosis — group II cancer sites

10-year survival per 1000 diagnosed*	Average annual death rate per 1000 survivors	Observed/expected deaths in the 12-month intervals following diagnosis						Sex and age at diagnosis	Cancer site	No. of cases at outset
		1st	2nd	3rd	4th	5th	6-10th (average)			
119	192	1.8	0.7	1.3	0.4	0.7	0.8	M 75+	Leukaemia, lymphoma	(153)
234	135	2.1	0.7	1.1	0.9	0.6	0.7	F 75+	Leukaemia, lymphoma	(82)
247	130	1.7	1.1	1.0	0.7	0.7	0.8	M 0-74	Leukaemia, lymphoma	(812)
312	110	2.2	1.4	0.6	0.7	0.8	0.6	F 0-74	Leukaemia, lymphoma	(512)
158	168	2.2	1.2	0.9	0.5	0.6	0.4	M 75+	Rectum	(538)
161	167	2.1	1.1	0.7	0.6	0.4	0.7	F 75+	Rectum	(319)
326	106	2.0	1.7	1.1	0.7	0.8	0.4	M 75+	Rectum	(2639)
437	79	2.3	1.7	1.2	0.9	0.6	0.4	F 75+	Rectum	(1149)
491	69	2.5	1.5	0.8	1.0	1.0	0.4	M 0-74	Hodgkin's	(660)
611	48	2.4	1.4	1.1	1.1	0.6	0.6	F 0-74	Hodgkin's	(378)
177	159	2.0	1.0	0.9	0.7	0.8	0.6	M 75+	Bladder	(743)
322	107	2.6	1.3	1.2	0.5	0.4	0.4	F 75+	Bladder	(238)
543	59	1.9	1.4	0.9	1.0	0.6	0.7	M 0-74	Bladder	(1894)
628	45	2.6	1.9	0.7	0.8	0.6	0.6	F 0-74	Bladder	(477)
231	136	2.0	1.5	0.8	0.6	—	0.5	M 75+	Melanoma	(55)
304	112	1.0	1.8	0.8	0.6	1.5	0.7	F 75+	Melanoma	(52)

Table D.7—Continued

10-year survival per 1000 diagnosed*	Average annual death rate per 1000 survivors	Observed/expected deaths in the 12-month intervals following diagnosis						Sex and age at diagnosis	Cancer site	No. of cases at outset
		1st	2nd	3rd	4th	5th	6-10th (average)			
554	57	1.8	1.9	1.3	1.0	1.0	0.4	M 0-74	Melanoma	(485)
714	34	1.7	1.6	1.4	0.9	1.1	0.6	F 0-74	Melanoma	(661)
203	147	2.8	1.0	0.9	0.8	0.3	0.3	F 75+	Cervix	(156)
635	44	2.0	2.1	1.5	0.5	0.7	0.4	F 0-74	Cervix	(2251)
300	113	2.0	0.9	1.1	0.7	1.2	0.6	F 75+	Uterus	(245)
753	28	2.1	1.6	1.1	1.0	0.6	0.7	F 0-74	Uterus	(2478)
707	34	3.0	1.8	1.1	0.6	0.4	0.5	M 0-74	Thyroid	(199)
873	13	1.2	1.0	0.3	0.6	0.2	0.9	F 0-74	Thyroid	(582)
Average		2.1	1.4	1.0	0.7	0.7	0.6			

* The *10-year survival* ('x') is the proportion of the original cases surviving 10 years after diagnosis. It is expressed here as the number remaining from 1000 cases living at the time of diagnosis.

**The *average annual death rate* ('d') is the annual rate which, if constant over the 10 12-month intervals following diagnosis, would result in the given 10-year survival. It is expressed here as the number of cases dying in any 12-month interval among 1000 survivors alive at the beginning of that interval. The proportion of these survivors dying in the succeeding 12 months ('d') is given by the expression

$$d = (1 - p) = [1 - (x^{1/10})]$$

where 'p' is the proportion surviving the 1-year period.

†The *expected deaths* ('d_n') in a particular one of the 12-month intervals following diagnosis are expressed here as per 1000 cases alive at the time of diagnosis. The proportion of this original cohort dying in the '*n*'th interval is given by the expression

$$d_n = p^{n-1} \cdot d.$$

Table D.8 Observed versus 'expected' deaths in successive 1-year periods following diagnosis — group III cancer sites

10-year survival per 1000 diagnosed*	Average annual death rate per 1000 survivors	Observed/expected deaths in the 12-month intervals following diagnosis						Sex and age at diagnosis	Cancer site	No. of cases at outset
		1st	2nd	3rd	4th	5th	6–10th (average)			
14	411	2.2	0.3	0.1	0.2	—	0.4	M 75+	Pancreas	(275)
30	296	2.9	0.4	0.2	0.1	0.1	0.3	M 0–74	Pancreas	(883)
45	267	3.1	0.5	0.1	0.2	—	0.1	F 0–74	Pancreas	(581)
69	234	3.6	0.4	0.1	—	—	—	F 75+	Pancreas	(179)
21	320	2.4	0.5	0.3	0.2	0.1	0.2	M 75+	Lung	(863)
82	221	3.0	0.9	0.3	0.2	0.2	0.2	M 0–74	Lung	(4673)
96	209	3.6	0.6	0.3	—	—	0.1	F 75+	Lung	(173)
156	170	3.4	1.1	0.5	0.2	0.2	0.1	F 0–74	Lung	(1068)
45	267	2.7	0.5	0.3	0.2	0.1	0.3	M 75+	Stomach	(581)
50	259	2.9	0.5	0.4	0.3	0.1	0.3	F 75+	Stomach	(319)
125	188	3.1	1.1	0.4	0.3	0.3	0.2	M 0–74	Stomach	(1923)
153	171	3.1	1.3	0.4	0.3	0.5	0.1	F 0–74	Stomach	(769)
183	156	3.2	1.1	0.4	0.3	0.3	0.3	M 0–74	Brain	(973)
217	142	3.4	1.0	0.5	0.3	0.3	0.3	M 75+	Brain	(594)
103	203	2.7	1.0	0.4	0.4	—	0.5	F 75+	Lymphosarcoma	(131)
160	167	2.6	1.4	0.6	0.4	0.2	0.4	M 75+	Lymphosarcoma	(99)
320	108	3.1	1.2	0.5	0.6	0.6	0.4	M 0–74	Lymphosarcoma	(812)
367	95	3.4	1.1	1.1	0.5	0.6	0.3	F 0–74	Lymphosarcoma	(512)
101	471	2.3	0.7	0.5	0.3	0.7	0.7	F 0–74	Kidney	(147)
194	380	2.5	1.0	0.7	0.6	0.8	0.4	F 75+	Kidney	(100)

Table D.8—Continued

10-year survival per 1000 diagnosed*	Average annual death rate per 1000 survivors	Observed/expected deaths in the 12-month intervals following diagnosis						Sex and age at diagnosis	Cancer site	No. of cases at outset
		1st	2nd	3rd	4th	5th	6–10th (average)			
343	298	3.0	1.2	0.8	0.6	0.4	0.5	M 0–74	Kidney	(966)
416	269	3.2	1.4	0.7	0.5	0.6	0.4	M 75+	Kidney	(543)
137	180	3.2	0.8	0.5	0.3	0.3	0.2	F 75+	Ovary	(163)
368	95	3.3	1.7	0.9	0.5	0.3	0.2	F 0–74	Ovary	(1651)
183	156	2.6	1.0	0.8	0.6	0.7	0.2	M 75+	L. intestine	(800)
231	136	2.7	0.9	0.8	0.8	0.3	0.6	F 75+	L. intestine	(847)
359	97	2.8	1.4	0.9	0.7	0.5	0.4	M 0–74	L. intestine	(2174)
423	82	2.9	1.7	0.9	0.7	0.5	0.3	F 0–74	L. intestine	(2324)
406	86	2.3	—	—	0.4	—	1.2	M 75+	Testis	(10)
782	24	3.8	2.5	1.1	0.6	0.1	0.3	M 0–74	Testis	(706)
Average		3.0	1.0	0.5	0.4	0.4	0.3			

* The *10-year survival* ('*x*') is the proportion of the original cases surviving 10 years after diagnosis. It is expressed here as the number remaining from 1000 cases living at the time of diagnosis.

** The *average annual death rate* ('*d*') is the annual rate which, if constant over the 10 12-month intervals following diagnosis, would result in the given 10-year survival. It is expressed here as the number of cases dying in any 12-month interval among 1000 survivors alive at the beginning of that interval. The proportion of these survivors dying in the succeeding 12 months ('*d*') is given by the expression

$$d = (1 - p) = [1 - (x^{1/10})]$$

where '*p*' is the proportion surviving the 1-year period.

† The *expected deaths* ('d_n') in a particular one of the 12-month intervals following diagnosis are expressed here as per 1000 cases alive at the time of diagnosis. The proportion of this original cohort dying in the '*n*'th interval is given by the expression

$$d_n = p^{n-1} \cdot d .$$

treat all of the remaining diagnoses as belonging to group II. It would then only be necessary to determine the relevant 10-year survivals.

In summary, the options open to anyone doing a death search initiated by cancer records are:

1. Use a crude approach in which the same average risk of death in a given year after diagnosis is applied regardless of the diagnosis.
2. Use the 'partial solution' in which the annual death rate among survivors is assumed to be constant over the first 10 years after the diagnosis. This will be specific for diagnosis, sex, and the age-group at the time of diagnosis.
3. Use, in addition to (2) above, an ADJUSTMENT FACTOR that corrects for the deviations from the assumed constant annual death rate.
4. Use the full life-table data, specific for diagnosis, sex, and the age-group at the time of the diagnosis, obtained from a very large register of cases.

The choice will depend on a trade-off between the level of accuracy and the effort invested in setting up the operation. However, where death searches are to be done routinely, the extra time devoted to increasing the accuracy is likely to be well spent if it reduces the later clerical effort of resolving ambiguous matches.

Appendix E:

Errors, their sources and magnitudes

Users and would-be users of record linkage vary in their require-ments for accuracy. To some, the immediate emphasis should be on simplicity rather than accuracy, in the hope of getting on with the job sooner. To others, who are concerned mainly with the measurement of mortality or morbidity, it may be sufficient that the false positives be balanced by an equal number of failures to achieve potential good links, if such a balance can be arranged. Only for a third group will a truly high level of accuracy be important. They will require that all potentially possible good linkages be implemented with a minimum of error of any kind. What all three sorts of users do have in common, however, is that each would like some measure of the quality of the product they are going to receive.

The purpose of Appendix E is therefore to explore the various causes of linkage errors, i.e. those of commission and those of omission, to see not only how they can be prevented but how they can be measured as well.

The sources of error are more diverse than is generally recognized:

1. The identifier(s) used for BLOCKING the files may disagree on some genuinely linkable pairs of records so that these are never brought together for comparison. The reason for this are various.
2. The *threshold* for acceptance or rejection of candidate pairs of records may be inappropriately placed so that the combined number of errors (false positives plus false negatives) is unnecessarily high.
3. There may be a *lack* of DISCRIMINATING POWER in the collective iden-tifiers common to a record pair, as when the date of birth is not fully stated.
4. There may be *underuse* of the DISCRIMINATING POWER inherent in the identifiers that are available, as when the comparison procedures recognize too few levels of outcome.
5. The identifiers may be *correlated* in some fashion with each other, as when a surname and given name are both characteristic of the same ethnic minority, or as when an informant makes multiple wrong guesses concerning the year, month, and day of birth.

6. There may also be an *imbalance* between the false-positive links and the failures to achieve potential good links. This is not simply a result of a wrongly placed threshold, because errors due to blocking may also contribute to the imbalance.

Each of these sources of error are now considered.

E.1. Choosing the 'best' blocking information

When the comparison pairs of records are limited to those sharing the same values of the sequencing or blocking information, potential good links may be missed due to discrepancies in the identifiers chosen for blocking. This is true whether some form of the surname is used, or a numerical identifier like the Canadian Social Insurance Number (SIN), or some other identifier or combination of identifiers such as the first given name plus the date of birth. It is unavoidable that the blocking information will at some time be differently assigned or recorded for the same individual.

The problem for the designer of a record linkage procedure is therefore that of minimizing the losses of potential good links, without at the same time incurring an unacceptable cost in terms of the numbers of record pairs that have to be examined. There may also be a requirement to assess these losses quantitatively, if that is possible. Moreover, much may depend on whether the searching is limited to just a single file sequence, or can be repeated in one or more alternative sequences using different sets of identifiers for the blocking. In this Section we consider the opportunities for reducing the losses due to blocking. (For convenience in the discussion it is assumed that the searching is done sequentially so that the terms 'sequencing information' and 'blocking information' are synonymous and can be used interchangeably.)

There is considerable confusion over what is meant by the 'best' blocking information. Both reliability and discriminating power need to be considered, and these are essentially independent characteristics of any identifier. Reliability serves to keep the losses down, and discriminating power is needed to keep the costs down. The definition of 'best' implies a balancing of one against the other.

Usually, some limit will have to be placed on the acceptable number of comparison pairs of records that must be examined by the computer to do a linkage job. Unless both files are small, this precludes the comparison of every search record with every record being searched. At the other extreme, a requirement for precise agreement of a battery of identifiers would often result in an unacceptably high number of errors in the form of missed linkages. The optimum lies somewhere in between.

Most frequently the sequencing of the files is based on some phonetically coded form of the surname, and there may be preferences concerning which code to use. Let us compare the two name codes that are most often employed. They are the NYSIIS code, which has already been discussed, and the Soundex code. The NYSIIS code is the more discriminating of the two. It breaks the file into smaller 'pockets', thereby reducing the numbers of comparison pairs of records and the central processor costs. The Soundex code, however, may be the more successful of the two at bringing together the discrepant forms of the surnames that are applied to the same individuals. If so, it will reduce the losses to a greater extent than will the NYSIIS code.

If an objective choice is to be made, both characteristics of both codes need to be quantified. Curiously, the comparison of the two characteristics at the same time does not seem to have been done elsewhere. So, by doing it here as an example we will acquaint the reader with a procedure that could be applied later to the comparison of any blocking system with any other. The procedure would also be profitably applied to any modifications of a coding system that are intended to improve it. It would, in effect, measure what has been gained in accuracy against what has been lost in terms of increased numbers of comparison pairs that the computer has to handle.

First let us compare the DISCRIMINATING POWERS of the NYSIIS and soundex surname codes. The procedure for measuring discriminating power is simple but the work can be tedious if done manually. What is sought is an indicator of the 'fineness' with which the file is divided by the identifier in question, namely a kind of 'average' pocket size. This will take the form of a weighted mean of all pocket sizes, expressed as a fraction of the total file. For a file that is being searched, such as a death file, the weightings for the different pockets should be in proportion to how often each of them is accessed during a search. Assuming that the file initiating the search is similar with respect to its division into pockets, the weightings will be in proportion to the sizes of the pockets being searched. Thus the weighted mean, or 'average', pocket size will be found by simply summing the squares of the individual pocket sizes (when these are expressed as fractions of the whole file). More formally, this is known as a COEFFICIENT OF SPECIFICITY.

COEFFICIENT OF SPECIFICITY = weighted 'average' pocket size
= sum of (the individual pocket sizes)^2

where pocket size is expressed as a fraction of the size of the whole file, and the summing is over all pockets in the file.

One may do the calculation either manually or by computer. If done manually, the labour can be reduced by grouping the frequency distribution into ranges of pocket sizes, as shown for the Soundex surname codes in Table E.1.

Table E.1 Calculating the coefficient of specificity of the Soundex surname code

No. of records with same code		No. of codes	Total records	Code frequency (%)	Frequency	Frequency × no. of codes
Size range	Midpoint (A)	(B)	(A × B)	(C)	($/10^4$) (C^2)	($/10^4$) ($B × C^2$)
1299	1299	1	1 299	1.0847	1.1766	1.1766
989	989	1	989	0.8259	0.6820	0.6820
790	790	1	790	0.6597	0.4352	0.4352
650– 749	700	3	2 100	0.5845	0.3417	1.0250
550– 649	600	9	5 400	0.5010	0.2510	2.2593
450– 549	500	7	3 500	0.4175	0.1743	1.2203
350– 449	400	21	8 400	0.3340	0.1116	2.3429
250– 349	300	26	7 800	0,2505	0.0628	1.6317
150– 249	200	90	18 000	0.1670	0.0279	2.5103
50– 149	100	377	37 000	0.0835	0.0070	2.6288
35– 49	42	211	8 862	0.0351	0.0012	0.2595
25– 34	30	194	5 820	0.0251	0.00063	0.1217
15– 24	20	354	7 080	0.0167	0.00028	0.0987
5– 14	10	974	9 740	0.0084	0.00007	0.0679
1– 4	2	1 487	2 974	0.0017	0.00003	0.0040
Sums		3 756	119 754			16.4639

Coefficient of specificity = 16.46/10^4 or 1/607.4

Table E.1 shows us that the surname Soundex code divides the file into the equivalent of 607 blocks of equal size, in other words each is equal to 0.165 per cent of the total file. The data are for surnames from the vital records of the Canadian province of British Columbia. These are not strictly comparable with the similar data available for the surname NYSIIS codes, which are based on death records for the whole of Canada. However, we will make the comparison anyway for purposes of illustration; the result is unlikely to be biased greatly.

What need to be known about these two blocking systems based on the SURNAME are the DISCRIMINATING POWERS of:

(1) the full *alphabetical* SURNAME;
(2) the NYSIIS coded form of the SURNAME;
(3) the information *excluded* by the NYSIIS;
(4) the Soundex coded form of the SURNAME, and
(5) the information *excluded* by the Soundex.

The reason for this kind of accounting is that each component of the discriminating power inherent in the full alphabetical surname will, if used in the blocking, be responsible also for some losses of potential good links. Clearly, the kind of specificity most needed is that associated with the fewest losses per unit of discriminating power. Conversely, the specificity to be excluded by the codings ought to be that which, if used, would be associated with a high ratio of losses to discriminating power. Numbers need to be attached to these ratios, because they constitute the only objective measure of quality on which to base the 'best' choice of blocking information. The principle is the same for any kind of identifier when used for this purpose.

For the NYSIIS and the Soundex codes the relevant data on DISCRIMINATING POWERS are as follows:

Component of the discriminating power	'Average' pocket size (as a fraction of the total file)
Full alphabetical SURNAME	1/2284
NYSIIS coded SURNAME	1/1148
Component *excluded* by NYSIIS	1/ 1.99
Soundex coded SURNAME	1/ 607
Component *excluded* by Soundex	1/ 3.76

The numbers for the 'excluded' components are obtained when the 'average' pocket size for the coded form of the surname is divided by the corresponding pocket size for the full alphabetical SURNAME. This may be viewed as the factor by which the full alphabetical information would typically subdivide the pockets created by the more limited coded information.

Having shown that use of the Soundex coded would roughly double the number of comparison pairs to be examined by the computer, as compared with the NYSIIS code, it remains to consider the losses of potential good links with the two systems. In other words, 'What is the trade-off between the level of "accuracy" versus the "cost" of achieving that level?' The comparison must be based on the frequencies with which the codes in question differ, or are unchanged, for discrepant pairs of surnames in the correctly linked record pairs. Use will be made of British Columbia data for birth records linked to parental marriage records and to sibling birth records. The multiple identifiers on these vital registrations make it possible to do the linkages even where a surname is in total disagreement. The data are shown in Table E.2.

The Soundex code appears from this test to be marginally more effective than the NYSIIS code in bringing together variant forms of the surnames:

Code	Proportion of differently spelled surnames brought together
NYSIIS	96/155 = 61.9%
Soundex	102/155 = 65.8%

This slight advantage of the soundex is clearly outweighed, however, by the substantially greater discriminating power of the NYSIIS.

It remains to quantify the 'quality' or 'merit' of the differently coded forms of the surname, and of the components excluded by the two codings. For this purpose it is convenient to express the DISCRIMINATING POWER in units which would double the number of pockets in a file that is equally divided, and halve the sizes of the pockets. Such units are logarithms to the base 2 of the inverse of the COEFFICIENT OF SPECIFICITY; in other words,

DISCRIMINATING POWER
$$= \log_2 [1/(\text{COEFFICIENT OF SPECIFICITY})].$$

Table E.2 Discrepancies of alphabetical surnames, and their NYSIIS and Soundex codes

Surname pairs		NYSIIS codes		Soundex codes		Numbers of pairs
Total matched pairs of surnames						7123
Total pairs in which the alphabetical spellings disagree						155
A. Both NYSIIS and Soundex agree (not listed here)						93
B. NYSIIS agrees, Soundex disagrees						3
PETERS	– PETER	PATAR	– PATAR	P 362	– P 360	
REGGINS	– REGINE	RAGAN	– RAGAN	R 252	– R 250	
REGGINS	– REGGINE	RAGAN	– RAGAN	R 252	– R 250	
C. NYSIIS disagrees, Soundex agrees						9
CARBATH	– CARVATH	CARBAT	– CARVAT	C 613	– C 613	
CROWTHERS	– CROWDER	CRATAR	– CRADAR	C 636	– C 636	
DETARGENY	– DETARJANY	DATARG	– DATARJ	D 362	– D 362	
ETZERZA	– ETZERTZA	ETSAR	– ETSART	E 326	– E 326	
GWYNUP	– GUYNUP	GYNAP	– GANAP	G 510	– G 510	
SCHMIDT	– SCHMITD	SNAD	– SNATD	S 530	– S 530	
SCHMITKE	– SCHMITHE	SNATC	– SNAT	S 253	– S 253	
SZENT	– SZENTMIKL	SANT	– SANTN	S 253	– S 253	
SZOZESIAK	– SZCZESIAK	S	– SC	S 222	– S 222	

Table E.2—Continued

Surname pairs	NYSIIS codes	Soundex codes	Numbers of pairs
D. NYSIIS disagrees, Soundex disagrees			50
ALDERMAN - ALOEMAN	ALDARN - ALARN	A 436 - A 465	
BARRO - BASIP	BAR - BASAP	B 600 - B 210	
BASCO - BOSCAR	BASC - BASCAR	B 200 - B 260	
BOESTERDD - DEN BOESTE	BASCAR - DANB	B 236 - D 512	
BOSA - ROSA	BAS - RAS	B 200 - R 200	
BRANTHAM - GRANTHAM	BRANT - GRANT	B 653 - G 653	
CARMICHAE - CALMICHAE	CARMAC - CALMAC	C 652 - C 452	
CHEZANECK - CHRZANECK	CASAN - CRSAN	C 252 - C 625	
COSTERD - LOSTERD	CASTAR - LASTAR	C 236 - L 236	
DION - PION	DAN - PAN	D 500 - P 500	
FINLAY - FINDLAY	FANLY - FANDLY	F 540 - F 534	
GAIR - CAIR	GAR - CAR	G 600 - C 600	
GATES - CATES	GAT - CAT	G 320 - C 320	
HAEUSER - HAEVSER	HASAR - HAVSAR	H 260 - H 126	
HOLT - HILL	HALT - HAL	H 430 - H 400	
HOOLEY - NOOLEY	HALY - NALY	H 400 - N 400	
HUCALA - CHALA	HACAL - CAL	H 240 - C 400	
HUEBSCHWE - HUCBSCHWE	HABSW - HACBSW	H 120 - H 212	
INTERMELA - ENTERMELA	INTARN - ENTARN	I 536 - E 536	
IWANYK - IVANICK	IANYC - IVANAC	I 520 - I 153	
IWANYK - IVANYK	IANYC - IVANYC	I 520 - I 152	
JENSEN - YENSEN	JANSAN - YANSAN	J 525 - Y 525	
KOCHN - KOEHN	CACHN - CAN	K 250 - K 250	
KRICK - KLICK	CRAC - CLAC	K 620 - K 420	
KURYLYK - KURYZYK	CARYLY - CARYSY	K 642 - K 620	

Table E.2—*Continued*

Surname pairs	NYSIIS codes	Soundex codes	Numbers of pairs
LAUMANN. – LAVMANN	LANAN – LAVAN	L 550 – L 155	
LEIMBECK – LEIMBELK	LANBAC – LANBAL	L 512 – L 514	
LUNGGREN – LJUNGGREN	LANGR – LJANGR	L 526 – L 252	
MAJALHTI – MAJALANTI	MAJALT – MAJAL	M 243 – M 245	
MILLEY – MILLER	MALY – MALAR	M 400 – M 460	
MOVAK – NOVAK	MAVAC – NAVAC	M 120 – N 120	
NACHBAR – NACNBAR	NACHB – NACNB	N 216 – N 251	
NIEDWIEC – NIED	NADW – NAD	N 320 – N 300	
NIESSEN – VONNIESSE	NASAN – VAN	N 250 – V 520	
OYTTERHAG – UTTERHAG	OTARAG – UTARAG	O 362 – U 362	
QUO – QUOVADIS	Q – QAVAD	Q 000 – Q 132	
PEMENT – DEMENT	PANANT – DANANT	P 553 – D 553	
PETKAU – PETKAV	PATC – PATCAV	P 320 – P 321	
POMRENKE – POMYENKE	PANRAN – PANYAN	P 565 – P 552	
PURVES – PURVER	PARV – PARVAR	P 612 – P 616	
RIEB – REID	RAB – RAD	R 100 – R 300	
ROMIJN – ROMAIN	RANAJN – RANAN	R 525 – R 550	
ROUALT – ROVAULT	RALT – RAVALT	R 430 – R 143	
SEGINOVIC – SZCZESUAJ	SAGAN – SC	S 251 – S 222	
SHIELDS – SHIEL	SALD – SAL	S 432 – S 430	
TITIRYN – TITISYN	TATARY – TATASY	T 365 – T 325	
TOOMES – TOOMBS	TAN – TANB	T 520 – T 512	
VERWEIG – VERWEY	VARWAG – VARWAY	V 620 – V 600	
WALLACE – KOWALSKI	WALAC – KALSC	W 420 – K 420	

The 'quality' or 'merit ratio' of any blocking information may be expressed in terms of the ratio of the DISCRIMINATING POWER it contains versus the likelihood of its *discrepancy* in correctly linked pairs of records. We use the percentage frequency for this likelihood. The 'merit ratio' is given by the expression;

MERIT RATIO
= (DISCRIMINATING POWER) / (% likelihood of discrepancy).

We may now quantify the 'merit' of the different sorts of blocking information in terms of this ratio, as shown in Table E.3.

The component of the SURNAME discriminating power that is extracted by a phonetic code of any kind is rather like high-grade ore in mining. What is left behind, for example the non-NYSIIS or non-Soundex component, is like the low-grade tailings from the mine. These still contain a little of the desired discriminating power, but it is now substantially diluted by the discarded tendency towards unwanted discrepancies.

If one were looking for an alternative kind of identification with which to do the BLOCKING, it is likely that the FIRST GIVEN NAME and the DATE OF BIRTH would be considered. On many work records that are used to initiate death searches, these are apt to be the only other identifiers consistently available for use. Much depends on the quality of this information as recorded in the files that are being linked to each other, but discrepancies are usually much more common than in the surnames. The treatment applied above to the

Table E.3 The merit of the components of the surname that may be used in blocking

Surname component	'Average' pocket size (A)	Specificity (B = 1/log₂ A)	Frequency of discrepancies (C)	Merit ratio (B/C)
Full alphabetical SURNAME	1/2284	11.16	155/7123 = 2.18%	5.1/1
NYSIIS	1/1148	10.16	59/7123 = 0.83%	12.2/1
Non-NYSIIS	1/ 1.99	0.99	96/7123 = 1.35%	0.7/1
Soundex	1/ 607	9.25	53/7123 = 0.74%	12.5/1
Non-Soundex	1/ 3.76	1.91	102/7123 = 1.43%	1.3/1

Table E.4 The merit of blocking information based on first given name and date of birth

Blocking component	'Average' pocket size (A)	Specificity $(B = 1/\log_2 A)$	Frequency of discrepancies (C)	Merit ratio (B/C)
FIRST GIVEN NAME	1/87	6.44	229/1262 = 18.15%	0.35/1
YEAR OF BIRTH	1/70	6.13	181/1072 = 16.88%	0.36/1
MONTH OF BIRTH	1/12	3.58	599/1059 = 11.71%	0.31/1
DAY OF BIRTH	1/30	4.91	150/1059 = 14.16%	0.35/1
Combined	1/2 192 400	21.06	48.44%*	0.43/1

* Assumes that the discrepancies are uncorrelated.

surname and its components is repeated here for these other identifiers using the example in Table E.4. These data are from an internal linkage of a work file; for linkages of the same work records with outside files the discrepancy rates could well be higher. The only likely use for blocking of such low quality would be to detect some fraction of the potential good links missed in an earlier search based on a better kind of sequencing information.

The treatment shown in Table E.4 may be applied also to an identifying number such as the Canadian Social Insurance Number or the US Social Security Number. These will certainly be discrepant from time to time on record pairs that are correctly linkable. However, the discriminating power of such a number is so great that the MERIT RATIO is likely to be exceedingly high.

We may now define what constitutes the 'best' blocking information. Where a limit is set on the cost of linkage, the blocking must obviously be fine enough to prevent the numbers of comparison pairs and the costs of handling them from becoming unacceptably high. Within that limitation, the information components selected for blocking should be those which together reflect a minimum of discrepancies in pairs that are correctly matched. These will be the components with the highest available MERIT RATIOS.

E.2. Estimating the losses from blocking

Various means have been devised for measuring or estimating the numbers of potential good links that are lost due to discrepancies in the blocking information. Mostly the approaches make use of extended searches or alternative searching sequences of the file that has already been scanned, or searches of some other file, or a combination of these. Manual extraction of information from records that have not been fully automated is a frequent ingredient. The most common limiting factors are the availability of a reserve of discriminating power, and the cost of the additional searches. Rarely is there a tidy and straightforward solution to the overall problem.

If it were not for costs, the ideal approach would be to compare every search record with every record in the file being searched. However, with large files this is usually out of the question. A next-best tactic is to carry out a search in two or more alternative blocking sequences using independent identifiers for each search. This has worked well where there was a second surname (e.g. a maiden name), or where a personal number (e.g. the Social Insurance or Social Security Number) could be used. Usually, however, one has to resort to whatever less tidy approach the circumstances permit. Two examples will illustrate this.

1. Use of a different file

In a follow-up of Ontario miners, an 'alive' search employing taxation records has been used to complement the death search. For those miners' records that contained the Social Insurance Number (SIN), this 'alive' search could be in numerical sequence, with the probabilistic feature of the procedure being used to spot occasional wrong SIN linkages. As well, among correct SIN linkages have been found surname discrepancies that cause the phonetic (i.e. NYSIIS) codings to differ. The limitations of both sorts of blocking information are thereby revealed; and these can be quantified, assuming simultaneous errors are not substantially more common than expected on chance alone.

2. Use of an extended search plus an alternative search sequence

In linkages of British Columbia birth record back to the parental marriage records, the main searching sequence was based on the father's surname plus the mother's maiden surname, both in Soundex coded form. The *extended search* that followed was then based on the father's surname code alone, ignoring the mother's but retaining the original file sequence. The *alternative search* was under the mother's surname code in a resequenced marriage file. (The result showed the alphabetical spellings of the fathers' and mothers' surnames to be discrepant, respectively, in 1 and 3 per cent of the correctly matched pairs; and the Soundex coded forms of the surnames were discrepant in 0.4 and 1.2 per cent of the pairs.)

The cost of such extended searches and alternative searches depends largely on whether a large proportion, or a small proportion, of the search records has to be subjected to this special treatment. The cost is least where the majority of the search records are expected to find true links in the file being searched. This is usually the case where the searches are for past records of a kind available for all members of a cohort, for example birth records or parental marriage records. Death searches, however, rarely fall into this category because usually many members of the cohort are still alive.

Some idea of the increase in 'wasted comparisons' when employing the above kind of approach may be gained from the example in Table E.5. This is concerned with the linkages of ill-health records and death records for children, back to the appro-

Table E.5 Numbers of comparison pairs of records versus the links, in file searches using extended and alternative blocking (records of ill health and death linked to birth records)

Blocking identifiers	No. of input records	No. of links	No. of comparison pairs per link
Soundex + DATE OF BIRTH	45 531	42 942	1.3
Soundex + FIRST GIVEN NAME	2 589	1 119	25
DATE OF BIRTH alone	1 470	487	289
Soundex + YEAR OF BIRTH	983	116	760
Still unlinked	867	—	—
Totals	45 531	44 664	

priate birth records, a study carried out by Miss Martha Smith using British Columbia records.

What made the approach illustrated in Table E.5 economically feasible was that the later searching steps involved such small proportions of the original search file. Each of the individuals presumably had a birth record; usually it was present and just had to be found. However, when applied to a death search in which many of the individuals would still be alive, the large numbers of search records that found no correct death link would continue to generate comparison pairs in each alternative blocking system and the cost-effectiveness would be reduced.

In general, tests to estimate the losses of good links due to blocking are necessarily opportunistic in nature. The discriminating power has to be there in a convenient form for the tests to be economical. Where this condition is met there is much that can be done. The most useful identifiers on which to base a blocking system secondary to that provided by the surname, in order of importance, are likely to be, (1) a personal number, (2) a second surname, or (3) the first given name plus the date of birth.

E.3. Thresholds as a source of error

A wrongly placed threshold for acceptance of matched pairs of records tends to increase the combined errors. In other words, it will increase the sum of the false positives plus false negatives.

The possible magnitudes of such errors may be investigated experimentally by linking files that are known to have been correctly linked earlier using other means. The prior linkage might be by an identifying number or, in the case of a death search, with the aid of a complementary 'alive' search plus clerical resolution of any conflicts, using information not available to the computer. However, where there is no prior knowledge of which record pairs are correctly matched and which are falsely matched, judgements concerning borderline cases are normally made subjectively and are prone to error.

Typical magnitudes of the errors with differently placed thresholds, as determined experimentally, are shown in Table E.6 for a typical death search based on 'good' identifying information. The Table gives some indication of the likely errors due to placing

Table E.6 Typical proportions of false positives and false negatives resulting from the choice of different thresholds for acceptance

Threshold (calculated absolute odds)	False positives (bad links gained) (%)*	False negatives (good links lost) (%)*	Total (false positives plus negatives) (%)*
1024/1	0.7	6.7	7.4
512/1	0.9	5.8	6.7
256/1	1.1	4.8	5.9
128/1	1.3	4.2	5.5
64/1	1.7	3.3	5.0
32/1	**2.1****	**2.8**	**4.9**
16/1	**2.7**	**2.0**	**4.7**
8/1	3.4	1.7	5.1
4/1	4.4	1.3	5.7
2/1	5.5	1.0	6.5
1/1	6.7	0.9	7.6
1/2	7.9	0.7	8.6
1/4	8.8	0.5	9.3
1/8	11.5	0.4	11.9
1/16	14.8	0.4	15.2
1/32	18.9	0.3	19.2

*Percentages based on the total potential good links.
**Figures in bold type indicate the approximate level of the 'best' threshold.

the threshold in other than the 'best' position. One might extrapolate from it to a linkage operation in which there is no prior knowledge of which pairs are correctly matched and which are falsely matched. However, such extrapolation would assume that the amount of identifying information in the search records, and its quality, were similar in the two situations. Where there is less discriminating power, the errors resulting from a misplaced threshold will be greater. Moreover, the optimum position for the threshold may vary with both the amount of discriminating power and the proportion of potentially linkable records in the search file.

It follows that the errors due to misplacing the threshold can often be estimated experimentally, but that care is needed to ensure strict comparability between the experimental and the actual situations when extrapolating from the one to the other.

In case this sounds unduly pessimistic, the reader should be reminded that both the problem and the solution hinge on the amount of combined discriminating power in the available identifying information. In a particularly favourable situation such as the linkage of infant death records back to the appropriate birth registrations, the problem becomes minuscule. Here there is more than just the child's name, date and place of birth to go on, because normally the records also have in common the mother's maiden surname, both parental given names, plus both parental places of birth. The collective discriminating power is enormous. As a result, the overlap between the calculated odds for the good matches and for the bad is minimal. The frequency distributions of the calculated odds is in this situation strongly bimodal, with a deep 'trough' at the 'optimum' threshold level. So, not only is there little uncertainty concerning the best position for the threshold, but the numbers of potential 'good' links and of actual 'bad' links falling on the wrong sides of the threshold are small.

In the less perfect situations commonly encountered, one may strive to optimize and to estimate the errors that could not be avoided, but the yield from such efforts will be more modest.

E.4. Lack of discriminating power as a source of error

A linkage operation is totally dependent for its success on the amount of discriminating power inherent in the identifiers that are common to the records being linked. However, little serious interest has been expressed in investigating the relationship quantitatively, despite the existence of large files of many kinds that are intended to be searched routinely, either by clerks or by machine.

This is unfortunate, because those who design the forms that make up such files are required to balance their own perceptions of the minimum requirement, against the perceptions of the informants and of the staff who actually gather the information. An objective basis would be desirable when deciding on the identifiers required by, for example, a cancer registry. 'Should the place of birth be asked for?' and 'Does one really need the month and day of birth, or would the year be sufficient?' These are the sorts of questions to which quantitative answers could be provided, given certain specified uses to which the records are likely to be put.

Table E.7 Typical proportions of false positives and false negatives resulting from the deletions of various identifiers

Identifiers used for linkage (in addition to the surname and first given name)	False positives (bad links gained) (%)*	False negatives (good links lost) (%)*	Total (false positives plus negatives) (%)*
1. Full DATE and PLACE OF BIRTH, plus the full MIDDLE NAME	3	3	6
2. Full DATE OF BIRTH	8	7	15
3. YEAR OF BIRTH (no month or day)	19	16	35
4. No DATE OF BIRTH information	—	95	95

* Percentages based on the total potential good links.

There are few if any relevant published statistics. However, a small unpublished study a few years ago yielded the tentative data shown in Table E.7, pertaining to a death search initiated by employment records.

An experiment to obtain similar data, systematically and in greater detail, is relatively simple to design. It would be based on an existing verified file of linked pairs of records, plus the falsely matched pairs that had been produced with them. From this file would be selected for use just those pairs in which a 'full set' of identifiers was present on both members of each correctly matched and falsely matched pair. The 'full set' might consist of the SURNAME and two GIVEN NAMES, the DATE OF BIRTH in full, and the PLACE OF BIRTH as the province, state, or foreign country of birth. The linkage would, in effect, be repeated with various identifiers 'removed' or 'suppressed', singly and in combination. In practice this would be a simple matter of recalculating the overall ABSOLUTE ODDS, after omitting the FREQUENCY RATIOS for the 'deleted' identifiers.

The success of such a test would depend on the inclusion of record pairs for which the original calculated odds extended downwards well below any plausible threshold. The reason for this requirement is that some of these falsely matched pairs could, when certain identifiers are 'suppressed' or 'removed' from them, have their calculated overall odds raised as a result. It is necessary therefore that they be represented at the outset, so that they have an opportunity to contribute to the subsequent false positives that are due to inadequate identifying information. Some experience with this kind of experiment has already been gained at Statistics Canada.

The effects of absences of key identifiers from the search records and from the records being searched will obviously vary from one linkage operation to another. When a search has been completed it is usual to list the resulting matched pairs of records in descending order of the calculated overall odds in favour of a correct link. The purpose of this is to permit visual scrutiny of the products to be concentrated on the borderline links which are thereby clustered together. A subjective impression is usually gained, in this manner, of the role played by missing identifiers in creating uncertainties. Such impressions provide valuable insights, but they are difficult to translate into objective data on error rates versus discriminating powers. It is for that reason that the experimental approach is favoured.

E.5. Underuse of discriminating power as a source of error

Underuse of discriminating power has the same effect on accuracy as lack of discriminating power. This is why emphasis has been placed on the need to recognize multiple levels and kinds of agreements, similarities, 'relatedness', dissimilarities, and more extreme disagreements. Only where there is an abundance of identification, or little need for accuracy, can one afford to be wasteful of discriminating power.

The value of recognizing multiple outcome levels is most apparent with such numerical identifiers as the DATE OF BIRTH components, and somewhat less so with the geographical identifiers such as PLACE OF WORK when compared with PLACE OF DEATH. But it extends even to disagreements of PLACE OF BIRTH, because understandable inaccuracies in these should not be confused with outright disagreements. A general rule applies in virtually all comparison procedures, which is that discriminating power is wasted whenever possible outcome levels, heterogeneous with respect to their FREQUENCY RATIOS, become pooled into a single level of outcome.

The point applies with special force to people's names. This is partly because so much discriminating power resides in them, and partly because of the many forms a particular name may take. It is true of the SURNAMES and more so of the GIVEN NAMES. Thus, effort is well spent when devoted to ensuring that the computer does not fail to recognize names similarities which are apparent to a manual searcher.

Series of outcome levels for the name comparisons have in the past been based mainly on the numbers of early characters that agree, and on whether the later ones disagree or are missing on one record as compared with the other. A suggested further refinement would use phonetically coded forms of the given names to reveal otherwise hidden similarities. Even dictionaries of nicknames and synonyms might be employed, although no convenient procedure has yet been developed.

There is a further possible approach that uses phonetic coding in a rather different way. Until now, the Soundex and NYSIIS codes have been applied mainly to 'block' the files, a function which *prevents* names with non-identical codes from being compared. An alternative is to *compare* the non-identical codes and use them to measure the *degree* of phonetic similarity.

The approach has been employed for the purpose of passenger airline bookings, in a system known as the '*ill-spelled name routine*'. What the routine does is to 'ignore' interruptions (i.e. insertions) in one or other, or both, members of an otherwise similar pair of phonetic sequences. Thus similar phonetic sequences are recognized despite the presence of 'foreign' or 'discrepant' elements.

The rules for the *ill-spelled name routine* are simple. Pairs of identical consonants are reduced to a single consonant, vowels are removed, and the result is truncated to four letters. The computer then looks to see if a code pair contains a three-letter sequence in common, regardless of whether that sequence is interrupted on one or both of the records. An example would be:

MCGINESS = *M C G N*
MAGINNES = *M G N* S.

The sequence 'M G N' is common to both of the above codes, under these rules. A lower level of similarity would be identified by a sequence of two letters in agreement under the same rules. In all, five levels of similarity/dissimilarity may be so defined. The treatment can be applied wherever the names are to be compared anyway, as in the case of given names when the surname codes already agree.

Estimates of the error rates due to underuse of discriminating power are best derived empirically. A desirable feature of such a test is the prior verification of the link/non-link status of the record pairs, by some other means. Visual examination of all borderline links will then provide evidence of the magnitude of the problem, which can be quantified by counting the similarities that the computer has failed to note. Where the associated linkage errors are numerous, devices for improving the accuracy such as those described above may be well worth the effort required for their development and implementation.

E.6. Correlated identifiers as a source of error

When FREQUENCY RATIOS are accumulated from the comparisons of the various identifiers in a matched pair of records it is assumed, as a convenient simplification, that each identifier is essentially independent of the others. This imlies uncorrelated likelihoods of agreement and disagreement, and also that the field values when they do agree are likewise uncorrelated. Where the assumption is false, the calculated overall ODDS in favour of a correct linkage may be biased either upward or downwards.

Such biases are generally thought to be small. This is because one can usually recognize in advance those identifiers that reflect essentially similar characteristics of the individual, and arrange the comparison procedure to avoid treating them as independent. Minor biases may remain, but these can be measured if one wishes. There are two kinds:

1. The simplest are due to *correlated discrepancies*. They probably arise mainly from multiple wrong guesses on the part of an informant. They could also occur where the person in question is the actual informant, but is confused or unwilling to give correct answers. The result is a downward bias.
2. The second kind is due to *correlated* AGREEMENT *values*. These are likely to occur in minority geographical and ethnic groups. Surnames, given names, and places of birth that are common enough within the group may be rare in the national context. Multiple agreements of these rare values will tend to acquire undue collective importance as

indicated by the accumulated value-specific FREQUENCY RATIOS. This bias is upward.

The magnitudes of both sorts of biases may be measured by comparing the observed with the expected numbers of multiple disagreements, or of multiple agreements of selected rare values.

The procedure is most simply illustrated in the case of the multiple disagreements. From a follow-up study of an occupational cohort, a modest sample of verified death linkages showed the frequencies of discrepancies in the YEAR, MONTH, and DAY OF BIRTH to be 26.0, 12.2, and 26.0 per cent respectively. From this could be calculated the expected numbers of record pairs containing discrepancies of 0, 1, 2, and 3 of these identifiers. A comparison of the observed with the expected numbers yielded the following results:

Number of discrepancies	Observed/expected nos. of record pairs
0	136/118.3 = 1.1
1	68/ 99.5 = 0.7
2	36/ 26.2 = 1.4
3	6/ 2.0 = 3.0

The bias due to the correlation may be seen from this simple test to be small as affecting those record pairs with 0, 1, or 2 discrepancies of the DATE OF BIRTH components. However, for the six record pairs which have triple discrepancies, the calculated overall ODDS in favour of linkage will be biased downwards by a factor of three. This might be sufficient to place these record pairs well below an optimum threshold when they ought correctly to be above it.

Application of a similar approach to estimate the upward bias from correlated agreement values is more complicated. Where particular surnames and given names are conspicuously common in a minority component of a study cohort, but are rare in the file being searched, their agreements ought correctly to carry less discriminating power when they occur together in the same record pair than when they occur separately. However, unless a special procedure is set up no such adjustment will be made.

An average measure of the magnitude of this source of bias may be obtained by distinguishing between names that have a 'local' or an 'ethnic' character and those that do not. Among the record pairs with simultaneous agreement of the surname plus the first given name, four combinations with respect to 'local' versus 'non-local' may be recognized. For each of these combinations the 'observed' frequency would then be compared with an 'expected' frequency based on an assumed random association. The anticipated bias in the case of the 'local–local' combination of agreements may be measured in this manner for a defined set of surnames and first given names.

Series of small empirical tests are quite adequate for such assessments of bias, but they do require thought as they progress. It is the feedback of data from the previous tests that should determine what the next small tests should be. Only those investigators seriously interested in the anatomy of the error properties of linked sets are likely to pursue this approach.

E.7. Imbalance between false positives and false negatives

The suggestion has been made that simplified linkage procedures might be adequate wherever the product is only to be used for statistical purposes. The idea is that an admixture of false-positive links and false-negatives would then be tolerable, provided they balanced one another out so the total was approximately correct. Costs might be reduced, and the manual verification of doubtful linkages avoided. Seemingly, all that is required is to place the threshold in the appropriate mid-position among the doubtful links. This notion deserves critical scrutiny, and so does an alternative solution.

The problem is to implement such a proposal. Unfortunately, the only way to ensure that the false positives and false negatives will indeed be in balance involves verifying individually as many of the doubtful links as possible, and assessing in addition the numbers of potential good links lost due to the blocking. This requires precisely the kind of labour that the proposal seeks to avoid. The work might perhaps be reduced by carrying it out on a sample of the files, and by applying the resulting 'best' threshold' to the full linkage operation. However, the success of any such approach will always be limited by the extent to which the true status of the borderline links can be verified, by clerical or other means. Where the identifying information is really inadequate, it is difficult to imagine a statistical treatment to take its place, even for the purpose of just balancing the false positives against the false negatives.

Fortunately, there is considerable experience with a convenient alternative. This is employed where the statistical product from a linkage study is intended to demonstrate some association, for example between particular occupations and excess deaths. The analysis is simply repeated using three different thresholds. Usually the middle one is chosen as the likely best, based subjectively on a visual examination of the linked pairs. The other two are deliberately placed too high and too low. If the same statistical associations hold for all three thresholds there will be strong assurance that they are real, and not due to imbalance between the false positives and false negatives.

This alternative has worked well, and no simple procedure has yet been devised for the proposed balancing of false positives and false negatives.

E.8. Assessing the overall errors in linked sets

Studies of the individual sources of linkage errors are of greater use as indicating opportunities for improving overall accuracy than as aiding in its assessment. Where actual measurement of overall accuracy is of special interest, this is best done directly using independent information concerning the true linkage status of the record pairs. In the absence of such independent verification, overall accuracy will always be imperfectly assessed.

Calculated overall ODDS do, however, serve to identify doubtful links in need of resolution. Moreover, from the numbers of these borderline links and the calculated ODDS, one does gain at least an idea of the approximate magnitude of the overall errors. Beyond that, various means may be employed to verify doubtful linkages and to determine where the linkage procedure has gone wrong. Visual scrutiny of borderline candidate pairs will sometimes reveal clues that the computer has not been instructed to recognize. Competing or conflicting alternative linkages may raise useful doubts, and clerically accessible information from records not available to the computer may tip the balance one way or the other. The often untidy process of visual assessment and 'manual resolution' can be based on any or all of these. Such resolutions and partial resolutions do say something about overall accuracy, but rarely is the resulting appraisal as quantitative as one would wish.

This is why the occasional opportunity to do a totally independent validity check is always of special interest. The most favourable situation is usually that in which an independent linkage can be based on a personal identity number. It matters little if the number is occasionally wrong because such instances are almost always easily spotted. What does matter is that not only the overall accuracy of the linkages gets revealed, but also the full breakdown into the components contributing to the errors. Other similar but less direct opportunities of this kind are provided by 'alive' searches to complement death searches, by the use of pension records for the same purpose, and by prior follow-up as confirming or conflicting with the results from a subsequent probablistic linkage, for example as in automated death clearance of cancer registry files where there is also a routine clerical follow-up. It is from such diverse sources that the best estimates of accuracy, and the best insights into the sources of inaccuracy, are obtained.

Where particularly favourable opportunities of the above kinds exist they should be exploited to the full. Moreover, the insights they provide should be documented and made available to others interested in the error properties of linked sets of records.

Appendix F:

Calculating the outcome frequencies for a non-existent file of unlinkable pairs

In the main text, emphasis has been placed on the use of an actual file of randomly matched UNLINKABLE pairs of records, wherever the frequencies of the various comparison outcomes in such a file are required to serve as denominators in the FREQUENCY RATIOS. In the past, the use of such an actual file has rarely been considered necessary because many of the outcome frequencies in it could be calculated instead.

Calculations of this kind are sometimes easy, sometimes not so easy, and sometimes far too complicated to be widely used in routine practice. One purpose of this Appendix is to describe the more important of these sorts of calculation so they can be employed by those who prefer not to create an actual file of UNLINKABLE pairs. A second purpose is to illustrate the various degrees of complexity of the calculations, so an informed choice can be made between the empirical and the theoretical approach.

We consider in particular the frequencies of various possible outcomes to do with,

(1) comparisons of the MONTH and DAY OF BIRTH;
(2) comparisons of the YEAR OF BIRTH;
(3) comparisons and cross-comparisons of INITIALS;
(4) agreements and partial agreements of NAMES.

F.1. Simple calculations for comparisons of month and day of birth

Where no actual file of UNLINKABLE pairs has been created, it is a relatively simple matter to calculate the expected frequencies of various levels of agreement, partial agreement, and more extreme disagreement of the MONTH and the DAY OF BIRTH in such a file.

Month of birth on work record

	J	F	M	A	M	J	J	A	S	O	N	D
J	0	+1	+2	+3	+4	+5	+6	+7	+8	+9	+10	+11
F	−1	0	+1	+2	+3	+4	+5	+6	+7	+8	+9	+10
M	−2	−1	0	+1	+2	+3	+4	+5	+6	+7	+8	+9
A	−3	−2	−1	0	+1	+2	+3	+4	+5	+6	+7	+8
M	−4	−3	−2	−1	0	+1	+2	+3	+4	+5	+6	+7
J	−5	−4	−3	−2	−1	0	+1	+2	+3	+4	+5	+6
J	−6	−5	−4	−3	−2	−1	0	+1	+2	+3	+4	+5
A	−7	−6	−5	−4	−3	−2	−1	0	+1	+2	+3	+4
S	−8	−7	−6	−5	−4	−3	−2	−1	0	+1	+2	+3
O	−9	−8	−7	−6	−5	−4	−3	−2	−1	0	+1	+2
N	−10	−9	−8	−7	−6	−5	−4	−3	−2	−1	0	+1
D	−11	−10	−9	−8	−7	−6	−5	−4	−3	−2	−1	0

Month of birth on death record (row labels)

Note: The frequencies of chance occurrences of various levels of agreement/disagreement of the MONTH OF BIRTH may be derived from the matrix by counting the relevant squares and dividing by the total squares (144). For example, the following frequencies may be obtained:

Discrepancy =	0 months	Frequency = 12/144 = 8.3%
Discrepancy = + or −	1 month	Frequency = 22/144 = 15.3%
Discrepancy = + or − 2 to 3 months		Frequency = 38/144 = 26.4%
Discrepancy = + or − 4 to 11 months		Frequency = 72/144 = 50.0%

The procedure can be adapted to comparisons of the DAY OF BIRTH by creating a 30 × 30 matrix and using it in the same fashion.

Births are assumed to be equally distributed over the months of the year and over the days of the month. There is a general formula that may be employed but the basis of the formula is best visualized in the form of a matrix. An example of such a matrix for comparisons of the MONTH OF BIRTH is given below; it relates to the comparisons of work records with death records. A similar but larger matrix could be employed in the same manner to obtain corresponding frequencies for different levels of outcome from comparisons of the DAY OF BIRTH.

The general formula with which to obtain the frequencies of various outcome levels, when the records are matched randomly, is:

$$\text{FREQUENCY OF DISCREPANCY } `x` = \frac{(n - x)}{n^2}$$

where 'n' is the number of months in a year (or days in a month), and 'x' is the magnitude of the positive difference, *or* of the negative difference, between the two different values of the month (or of the day of the month). If both positive and negative differences are to be included together, the amount $(n - x)$ must be multiplied by 2.

Slight seasonal differences in the distributions of births throughout the year have only trivial effects on the accuracy of the calculation. In practice, the formula yields almost precisely the same outcome frequencies as are found in an actual file of UNLINKABLE pairs that have been matched at random.

F.2. Less simple calculations for comparisons of year of birth

Calculation of the frequencies of chance occurrences of the possible levels of outcome from comparisons of the YEAR OF BIRTH (i.e. among UNLINKABLE pairs) is complicated by the unequal distributions of births throughout the calendar years, in the two files being linked. The procedure must therefore differ from those used for comparisons of the month and of the day of birth. To simplify the present treatment we will consider first the precise agreements of YEAR OF BIRTH, and then deal separately with the partial agreements.

The principle is obvious. For a particular calendar YEAR OF BIRTH, the frequency with which there will be a precise agreement by pure chance, among all the products from random pairings between the two files, will be equal to the frequency of that year as found in the search file, *times* the corresponding frequency in the file being searched. Moreover, where the year itself is unimportant, a value non-specific frequency may be obtained from the frequencies of precise agreements for the individual years by summing them over all years of birth.

The procedure is illustrated in Table F.1 in a form that lends itself to manual calculation. To minimize the preparation of the Table, the calendar years of birth have been grouped into decades, and the

Table F.1 Calculation of the frequencies of chance precise agreements of year of birth among random pairings of work records with death records (the example relates to a search of just the 1979 death file)

Ranges of years of birth (decades)	Corresponding age-ranges in 1979	For a single average year of birth within each decade of birth		
		Percentage frequency in the death records (*A*)	Percentage frequency in the work records (*B*)	Frequency per 10 000, for precise agreements in an average year of each decade (*A* × *B*)
1870–9	100–109	0.02	0.02	0.0004
1880–9	90– 99	0.47	0.06	0.0282
1890–9	80– 89	1.80	0.21	0.3780
1900–9	70– 79	2.36	0.60	1.4160
1910–19	60– 69	2.07	1.02	2.1114
1920–9	50– 59	1.28	2.35	3.0080
1930–9	40– 49	0.64	2.23	1.4272
1940–9	30– 39	0.27	1.55	0.4185
1950–9	20– 29	0.31	1.69	0.5390
1960–9	10– 19	0.23	0.27	0.0621
1970–9	0– 9	0.55	0.00	0.0000
Sums over all years in all decades		100.00%	100.00%	$93.8880/10^4$

frequencies given in a particular line are those for an average year in that decade. The example relates to an occupational cohort, and to the death searches pertaining to just a single year of deaths (1979). The advantage of doing death searches in this manner, i.e. conceptually, has been discussed in the main text. (p. 88).

Where the same kind of calculation is to be carried out by computer it is best done separately for each calendar YEAR OF BIRTH, instead of just for an average year within each decade.

The corresponding frequencies for PARTIAL AGREEMENTS may be obtained in essentially the same fashion. With small discrepancies of exact amounts, such as $+3$ years or -5 years, the frequencies should not differ greatly from those of the precise AGREEMENTS. Usually, however, one will want to define a level of PARTIAL AGREEMENT in terms of a range, such as a difference of $+$ or $-$ 3 to 5 years. In this case the expected frequency for the range will be the sum of the frequencies of the individual exact DISAGREEMENTS. For example, with the range of $+$ or $-$ 3 to 5 years the frequency of all differences falling within the range as a whole will be about six times the collective frequency of all the precise AGREEMENTS. With larger discrepancies such as $+10$ or -10 years, one might want to set up a table similar to Table F.1 but arranged specifically to calculate the exact frequency of the difference one had in mind (e.g. $+10$ years, with a separate table for -10 years).

These calculations ought to be repeated for each new linkage operation, wherever a new search file (or a new file to be searched) is being used.

In the example shown in Table F.1:

1. The chance of a *specified* year of birth agreeing, when the search record *already carries that year of birth*, is given in column (A).
2. The overall chance of a precise agreement of the year of birth (i.e. any year, *unspecified*) equals the sum of the products in the final column, i.e. summed over all years of all decades. In the present example, the frequency of this value non-specific, 'global' agreement outcome = $93.8880/10^4$, or 0.94 per cent.
3. The chance of a disagreement of, say, $+1$, $+2$, $+3$, $+4$, or $+5$ (*or* of -1, -2, -3, -4, or -5) will not differ greatly from the chance of a precise agreement. For ranges of disagreement levels, the frequencies will be obtained by summing those for the individual levels.

F.3. Comparisons and cross-comparisons of initials

Calculating the frequencies of fortuitous agreements and disagreements of FIRST and SECOND INITIALS, when compared directly and also cross-compared in a single procedure, is a tedious but straightforward task.

The number of possible outcomes is substantial when all missing initials are taken into account, but can be considerably reduced by ignoring records with a missing first initial. (A second initial, when present, may be moved into a vacant first position; and, where both the first and the second are absent, no comparison is needed.) The logic may be further simplified by considering separately the record pairs in which both initials are present, in which the second initial is absent from a search record (record A), in which it is absent from a record being searched (record B), and in which it is absent from both.

We refer to the first and second initials on record A as 'A1' and 'A2', and those on record B as 'B1' and 'B2'. For a given pair of records, the initials are compared in a total of four ways:

(1) first initial, straight compared:—   A1–B1;
(2) second initial, straight compared:—   A2–B2;
(3) first cross-comparison:—   A1–B2;
(4) second cross-comparison:—   A2–B1.

These four simultaneous comparisons may be referred to as 11, 22, 12, and 21 respectively. The comparison outcome as a whole will take all four 'sub-outcomes' into account. There are three possible sub-outcomes: AGREEMENT, DISAGREEMENT, and blank (i.e. one or both initials missing). Thus, the full set of comparisons and cross-comparisons of the two initials together create a maximum of $3^4 = 81$ possible combined outcomes. However, not all of these can actually occur.

Grouping by presence or absence of the second initial

The problem is broken down by arranging the possible outcomes into four groups, based on the numbers and locations of blank INITIALS in the comparison pairs of records. The groups may be defined as follows, with respect to presence or absence of the SECOND INITIAL:

(1) Group A: SECOND INITIAL present on both records;
(2) Group B: SECOND INITIAL missing from record A, present on record B;
(3) Group C: SECOND INITIAL present on record A, missing from record B;
(4) Group D: SECOND INITIAL missing from both records.

The frequencies of occurrence of these four groups among

randomly matched pairs of records may be calculated from the
frequencies of missing SECOND INITIALS in the respective files
being linked (files A and B). For example, let us assume the
following frequencies of presence and absence of the SECOND
INITIAL on the records for an occupational cohort (file A), and on
those for a death file that is being searched (file B):

File A
   (occupational cohort)   SECOND INITIALS present 62% $(= 1 - x)$;
                                   SECOND INITIALS absent   38% $(= \quad x)$;
File B (death records)   SECOND INITIALS present 77% $(= 1 - y)$;
                                   SECOND INITIALS absent   23% $(= \quad y)$.

In random pairings of the work records with the death records the
frequencies of the four outcome groups will be:

Group A: SECOND INITIAL
          present on both,   frequency $= (1 - x)(1 - y) = 47.7\%$;
Group B: SECOND INITIAL
          missing from record A,   frequency $= x(1 - y)$ $= 29.3\%$;
Group C: SECOND INITIAL
          missing from record B,   frequency $= y(1 - x)$ $= 14.3\%$;
Group D: SECOND INITIAL
          missing from both,   frequency $= xy$ $= 8.7\%$.

We may now consider the frequencies of the outcomes *within* the
groups.

Group A: second initial present on both records   In this group there
are *two* INITIALS on every record; so, for a given record pair these
will be compared simultaneously in four ways (11, 22, 12, 21). An
outcome may then be represented by four AGREEMENTS, four
DISAGREEMENTS, or various combinations of four such 'sub-
outcomes'. There are thus $2^4 = 16$ formal possibilities to consider,
but only 12 of these can actually occur. Our task is to determine their
frequencies when the records are randomly paired.

    The logic is straightforward for two reasons. First, the probability
that an initial will agree by pure chance is known, and is taken to be a
constant. Second, there are only four comparison steps in the chain
of reasoning (11, 22, 12, 21), and only two possible 'sub-outcomes'
at each step (AGREEMENT or DISAGREEMENT). This creates a
bifurcating pathway, Moreover, the logic closely resembles the
workings of the human mind when doing the job manually.

    At each point in the reasoning, when an initial is compared in any fashion, one must consider the likelihood of a fortuitous AGREEMENT versus that of a fortuitous DISAGREEMENT. For purposes of illustration we will use previously quoted values for these as indicated below:

Probability of a fortuitous AGREEMENT $= 6.9\% (= p)$
Probability of a fortuitous DISAGREEMENT $= 93.1\% (= q = 1 - p)$.

These probabilities ('p' and 'q') are accumulated over the four successive steps in the reasoning, as illustrated in Fig. F.1. Information from similar diagrams for groups A to D is summarized at the end of this Section.

Group B: Second initial missing from record A, present on record B In group B, search records (record A) lack second initials and matching records (record B) have them. Comparisons and cross-comparisons (11, 22, 12, 21) yield 'sub-outcomes' that are AGREEMENTS, DISAGREEMENTS, or BLANKS (i.e. initial missing on one record); but the combinations are limited because, of the four possible comparison, A1–B1 and A1–B2 *cannot*, and A2–B2 and A2–B1 *must*, yield 'blanks' (Fig. F.2).

Group C: Second initial present on record A, missing from record B The comparison patterns for groups B and C are similar, except that the last two columns are reversed (see Fig. F.3).

Group D: Second initial missing from both records Within group D, both records of a pair lack a second initial. Only the first initials can usefully be compared (comparison 11), and the only sub-outcomes from this are either AGREEMENTS or DISAGREEMENTS; all the other comparisons would have blank sub-outcomes. The frequencies within the group are obvious (Fig. F.4).

Combining the information on outcome frequencies into a compact and usable form

It remains to define a compact and convenient set of overall outcomes from the simultaneous straight- plus cross-comparisons of the INITIALS. This involves a regrouping on the basis of (1) the total number of AGREEMENTS plus DISAGREEMENTS (4, 2, or 1),

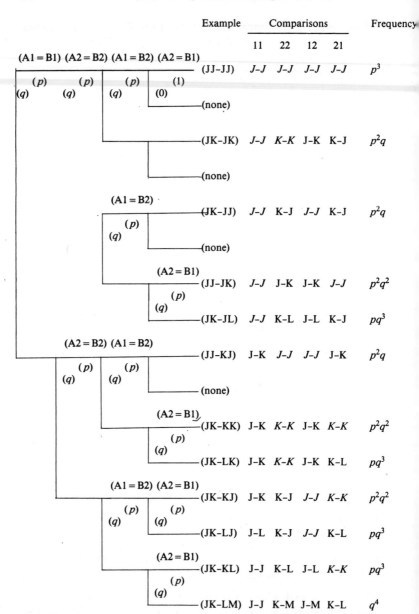

Fig. F.1

Example	Comparisons				Frequency
	11	22	12	21	

(A1 = B1) (A1 = B2)
 (p) (p)
(q) (q)

(J♭–JJ)	J–J	♭–J	J–J	♭–J	p^2
(J♭–JK)	J–J	♭–K	J–K	♭–J	pq

(A1 = B2)
 (p)
(q)

(J♭–KJ)	J–K	♭–J	J–J	♭–K	pq
(J♭–KL)	J–K	♭–L	J–L	♭–K	q^2

Fig. F.2

Example	Comparisons				Frequency
	11	22	12	21	

(A1 = B1) (A2 = B1)
 (p) (p)
(q) (q)

(JJ–j♭)	J–J	J–♭	J–♭	J–J	p^2
(JK–J♭)	J–J	K–♭	J–♭	K–J	pq

(A2 = B1)
 (p)
(q)

(JJ–K♭)	J–K	K–♭	J–♭	K–K	pq
(JK–L♭)	J–L	K–♭	J–♭	K–L	q^2

Fig. F.3   Second initial missing from record B

Example	Comparisons				Frequency
	11	22	12	21	

(A1 = B1)
 (p)
(q)

(J♭–J♭)	J–J	♭–♭	J–♭	♭–J	p
(J♭–K♭)	J–K	♭–♭	J–♭	♭–K	q

Fig. F.4   Second initial missing from records

and within these by (2) the SIMILARITIES of the frequencies, i.e. by
the number of AGREEMENTS alone (4, 2, 1, 0).

This regrouping is made more compact because the random
chance of an initial *disagreeing* is close to unity, in other words in the
vicinity of 0.93. This means that the calculated outcome frequencies

Table F.2 Outcome levels and frequencies for simultaneous comparisons and cross-comparisons of initials, with examples

Outcome level	Calculated frequency*		example**
Four AGREEMENTS/DISAGREEMENTS			
Group frequency	$(1-x)(1-y)$		$= 47.7\%$
Within-group frequencies:			
4 agree + 0 disagree	(p^3)	$= 0.03\%$	
2 agree + 2 disagree	$3(p^3q) + 3(p^2q^2)$	$= 2.6\%$	
1 agree + 3 disagree	$4(pq^3)$	$= 22.3\%$	
0 agree + 4 disagree	(q^4)	$= 75.1\%$	
Two AGREEMENTS/DISAGREEMENTS			
Group frequency	$x(1-y) + y(1-x)$		$= 43.6\%$
Within-group frequencies:			
2 agree + 0 disagree	(p^2)	$= 0.5\%$	
1 agree + 1 disagree	$2(pq)$	$= 13.0\%$	
0 agree + 2 disagree	(q^2)	$= 86.5\%$	
One AGREEMENT/DISAGREEMENT			
Group frequency	xy		$= 8.7\%$
Within-group frequencies:			
1 agree + 0 disagree	(p)	$= 6.9\%$	
0 agree + 1 disagree	(q)	$= 93.1\%$	

*See definitions of x, y, p, and q in text. (p. 161 and below).
**See p. 160 and below.

p^3q and p^2q^2 differ by only a factor of 0.93, and may be pooled without introducing more than trivial heterogeneity.

The regrouped outcomes are shown in Table F.2, together with the examples mentioned earlier. The variables are:

$x = 38\%$ = frequency of blank second initial on search records;
$y = 23\%$ = frequency of blank second initial on records being searched;
$p = 6.9\%$ = frequency of chance agreement of an initial;
$q = 93.1\%$ = frequency of chance disagreement of an initial.

The levels of outcome are defined in Table F.2 by the numbers of AGREEMENT and DISAGREEMENT sub-outcomes, regardless of whether these are from the straight- or the cross-comparisons. Blank sub-outcomes are ignored, but their inclusion must always bring the total to 4. The number of outcome levels defined in the Table is not excessive for routine use. When calculating FREQUENCY RATIOS, both the *group* frequencies and the *within-group* frequencies would contribute; the simplest procedure is to multiply the one by the other.

With a succession of linkage jobs the group frequencies would need to be recalculated whenever the files changed. This is because of likely differences in the use or non-use of a second initial. Calculation of the group frequencies is fortunately not time consuming.

The within-group frequencies are apt to be more stable and less likely to require recalculation. Only for local studies in which ethnic minorities may alter the frequencies of the various initials, and the frequency distribution, would the within-group frequencies be expected to differ greatly from the norm.

F.4. Agreements and partial agreements of given names

For the comparisons of *GIVEN* NAMES it is prudent to recognize a wide range of partial agreement and partial disagreement outcomes. The reason is that these identifiers contribute a major part of the overall discriminating power, and much of this contribution would remain hidden from the computer if the similarities between differently reported versions of the same name were not taken into account. Calculation of the frequencies of the various outcomes in UNLINKABLE pairs is complicated by the number of logical distinctions that ought to be made in the interests of refinement. However, the calculation process can be kept straightforward and unconfusing provided short cuts are avoided.

The levels of outcome suggested in the main text are based on:

(1) the *number of characters* at the beginning of the name that *agree*;
(2) whether there is a FULL AGREEMENT;
(3) whether the agreement portion is followed by a *truncation* on one of the records, with no disagreement of the actual characters;
(4) whether the agreement portion is followed by a partial DISAGREEMENT, i.e. of one or more characters.

Calculation of the outcome frequencies depends therefore on a knowledge of both the *lengths* of the names being compared, and the *likelihoods* of AGREEMENT of various numbers of characters when the comparisons are made. These two ingredients are considered separately.

The first step is to determine how often names of various lengths will be compared with each other when brought together at random. To simplify this step is is convenient to limit the lengths of the names being compared to a maximum of 7 characters. The total number of possible combinations by size will therefore be $7^2 = 49$, where the distinction is retained between the search records and the records being searched. An example will illustrate the manner in which actual frequencies would be handled. In the example chosen, the percentages of records with various numbers of characters are taken to be:

7 (11%), 6 (22%), 5 (25%), 4 (21%), 3 (20%), 2 (1%), and 1 (0%).

We will assume also that the two files are identical in this respect. (In actual practice they need not be, as when an employment list using informal given names is used to search a death file containing largely the unabbreviated versions of these.) The possible random combinations of name lengths and the frequencies of these in our example are shown in Fig. F.5. The letters in the Figure indicate the search file (A), and the file being searched (B); the numbers (7 to 1) indicate the total letters in the given name from the particular file.

Record pairs falling in the various cells of the matrix shown in Fig. F.5 differ from cell to cell with respect to the comparison outcomes that are possible. For example, FULL AGREEMENT of a name on a record pair is possible only where the number of letters is the same; such pairs are represented in the cells of the diagonal A7, B7 to A1, B1. Conversely, a relative *truncation* is *not* possible in these record pairs; it may only occur where there is a difference in name length and all of the characters of the shorter version agree. There are other constraints: for example, the number of characters agreeing cannot exceed the number in the name with the fewer characters; also, the agreement portion of a mixed AGREEMENT plus DISAGREEMENT must have at least one less character than the name with the fewer characters. So, for each cell in the matrix there is a defined set of possible outcomes.

Given the possibility of an agreement (or non-agreement) of a specified number of characters, the 'general' (i.e. value non-specific) frequency of such agreements may be applied. The manner in which these general frequencies are obtained from the files has already

File being searched

	B7 (11%)	B6 (22%)	B5 (25%)	B4 (21%)	B3 (20%)	B2 (1%)	B1 (0%)
A7 (11%)	A7,B7 (1.21%)	A7,B6 (2.42%)	A7,B5 (2.75%)	A7,B4 (2.31%)	A7,B3 (2.20%)	A7,B2 (0.11%)	A7,B1 (0.00%)
A6 (22%)	A6,B7 (2.42%)	A6,B6 (4.84%)	A6,B5 (5.50%)	A6,B4 (4.62%)	A6,B3 (4.40%)	A6,B2 (0.22%)	A6,B1 (0.00%)
A5 (25%)	A5,B7 (2.75%)	A5,B6 (5.50%)	A5,B5 (6.25%)	A5,B4 (5.25%)	A5,B3 (5.00%)	A5,B2 (0.25%)	A5,B1 (0.00%)
A4 (21%)	A4,B7 (2.31%)	A4,B6 (4.62%)	A4,B5 (5.25%)	A4,B4 (4.41%)	A4,B3 (4.20%)	A4,B2 (0.21%)	A4,B1 (0.00%)
A3 (20%)	A3,B7 (2.20%)	A3,B6 (4.40%)	A3,B5 (5.00%)	A3,B4 (4.20%)	A3,B3 (4.00%)	A3,B2 (0.20%)	A3,B1 (0.00%)
A2 (1%)	A2,B7 (0.11%)	A2,B6 (0.22%)	A2,B5 (0.25%)	A2,B4 (0.21%)	A2,B3 (0.20%)	A2,B2 (0.01%)	A2,B1 (0.00%)
A1 (0%)	A1,B7 (0.00%)	A1,B6 (0.00%)	A1,B5 (0.00%)	A1,B4 (0.00%)	A1,B3 (0.00%)	A1,B2 (0.00%)	A1,B1 (0.00%)

(Left margin label: S e a r c h F i l e)

Fig. F.5 Random combinations of given names of different lengths

been described (p. 29). For our example we will use the following frequencies and will rearrange the cells of the matrix of Fig. F.5 as shown in Table F.3.

No. of characters agreeing	General frequency (%)		Differences	(%)
7 or more	$p_7 =$	1.146	7 only p_7 =	1.146
6 or more	$p_6 =$	1.180	6 only $p_6 - p_7$ =	0.034
5 or more	$p_5 =$	1.227	5 only $p_5 - p_6$ =	0.047
4 or more	$p_4 =$	1.287	4 only $p_4 - p_5$ =	0.060
3 or more	$p_3 =$	1.469	3 only $p_3 - p_4$ =	0.182
2 or more	$p_2 =$	2.635	2 only $p_2 - p_3$ =	1.166
1 or more	$p_1 =$	7.299	1 only $p_1 - p_2$ =	4.664
0 or more	$p_0 =$	100.000	0 only $p_0 - p_1$ =	92.701

Before the examples of the probabilities are filled in to make a usable table, a further rearrangement is needed to group the outcomes into three categories — FULL AGREEMENT, AGREEMENT plus *truncation*, and AGREEMENT plus DISAGREEMENT. Within these groupings the outcomes will be arranged in descending order of the number of characters that agree. Here, the percentages represented by the three categories of outcome will sum to more than 100. This is because, for most of the comparison pairs, there will be a number of possible levels of agreement as indicated in Table F.3. The further rearrangement is shown in Table F.4.

Table F.4 is usable but unnecessarily large for the practical purpose of calculating FREQUENCY RATIOS. There is no special reason to have the FULL AGREEMENTS broken down by the number of characters that agree. For the other two categories, the agreements of 4, 5, and 6 characters carry essentially similar discriminating powers and could well be combined. Moreover, it is usually best at this stage to exclude comparisons involving initials alone, and to consider only those name pairs in which there are at least two characters to be compared and the initials already agree. Table F.5 contains a more compact and convenient version of the essential information for this purpose.

The chief disadvantage of this kind of calculation is the amount of labour involved. Where linkages are carried out routinely on a succession of files that differ substantially from one another, the temptation to use old numbers repeatedly is difficult to resist. This is not good, and the reader is advised to consider carefully the alternative of deriving the frequencies from an actual file of UNLINKABLE pairs created for each new job.

F.5. Agreements and partial agreements of surnames

For the comparisons of SURNAMES the desired number of partial agreement and partial disagreement outcomes may be somewhat less than for given names. (Surnames, although variable, are perhaps less so than given names.) However, it is unwise to assume that this should simplify calculation of the outcome frequencies expected in UNLINKABLE pairs. Short cuts involve pitfalls so the full procedure is best.

The levels of outcome suggested in the main text are defined as follows:

1. FULL AGREEMENT implies that the NYSIIS code agrees, that all

Table F.3 Matrix information (Fig. F.5) rearranged in order of the number of letters that can be compared

Nos. of characters in the two names	% of all pairs (example from Fig. F.5)	cumulative	Probabilities of various numbers of letters agreeing							
			7	6	5	4	3	2	1	0
7, 7	1.21	1.21	p_7^*	p_6-p_7	p_5-p_6	p_4-p_5	p_3-p_4	p_2-p_3	p_1-p_2	p_0-p_1
6, 6	4.84	10.89	—	p_6^*	p_5-p_6	p_4-p_5	p_3-p_4	p_2-p_3	p_1-p_2	p_0-p_1
6, 7	4.84		—	p_6^{**}	p_5-p_6	p_4-p_5	p_3-p_4	p_2-p_3	p_1-p_2	p_0-p_1
5, 5	6.25	33.64	—	—	p_5^*	p_4-p_5	p_3-p_4	p_2-p_3	p_1-p_2	p_0-p_1
5, 6+	16.50		—	—	p_5^{**}	p_4-p_5	p_3-p_4	p_2-p_3	p_1-p_2	p_0-p_1
4, 4	4.41	62.41	—	—	—	p_4^*	p_3-p_4	p_2-p_3	p_1-p_2	p_0-p_1
4, 5+	24.36		—	—	—	p_4^{**}	p_3-p_4	p_2-p_3	p_1-p_2	p_0-p_1
3, 3	4.00	98.01	—	—	—	—	p_3^*	p_2-p_3	p_1-p_2	p_0-p_1
3, 4+	31.60		—	—	—	—	p_3^{**}	p_2-p_3	p_1-p_2	p_0-p_1
2, 2	0.01	100.00	—	—	—	—	—	p_2^*	p_1-p_2	p_0-p_1
2, 3+	1.98		—	—	—	—	—	p_2^{**}	p_1-p_2	p_0-p_1
1, 1	0.00	100.00	—	—	—	—	—	—	p_1^*	p_0-p_1
1, 2+	0.00		—	—	—	—	—	—	p_1^{**}	p_0-p_1

*Full agreements are possible with these, but not with the others.
**Relative truncations are possible with these, but not with the others.

Table F.4 Matrix information (Fig. F.5) rearranged again, by category of outcome, and in descending order of the number of letters that agree

Nos. of characters that agree	Nos. of characters available on the two records	% of the record pairs involved (example) (C)	% probability of that level of agreement (example) (P)	Combined probability per 10 000 among all record pairs (C × P)
Exact AGREEMENT				
7	7, 7	1.21	p^7 = 1.146	1.386 66
6	6, 6	4.84	p^6 = 1.180	5.711 20
5	5, 5	6.25	p^5 = 1.227	7.668 75
4	4, 4	4.41	p^4 = 1.287	5.675 67
3	3, 3	4.00	p^3 = 1.469	5.876 00
2	2, 2	0.01	p^2 = 2.635	0.026 35
1	1, 1	0.00	p^1 = 7.299	0.000 00
AGREEMENT plus truncation				
6	6, 7	4.84	p^6 = 1.180	5.711 20
5	5, 6+	16.50	p^5 = 1.227	20.245 50
4	4, 5+	24.36	p^4 = 1.287	31.351 32
3	3, 4+	31.60	p^3 = 1.469	46.420 40
2	2, 3+	1.98	p^2 = 2.635	5.217 30
1	1, 2+	0.00	p^1 = 7.299	0.000 00
AGREEMENT plus DISAGREEMENT				
6	7, 7	1.21	$p^6 - p^7$ = 0.034	0.041 14
5	6+, 6+	10.89	$p^5 - p^6$ = 0.047	0.511 83
4	5+, 5+	33.64	$p^4 - p^5$ = 0.060	2.018 40
3	4+, 4+	62.41	$p^3 - p^4$ = 0.182	11.358 62
2	3+, 3+	98.01	$p^2 - p^3$ = 1.166	114.279 66
1	2+, 2+	100.00	$p^1 - p^2$ = 4.664	466.400 00
0	1+, 1+	100.00	$p^0 - p^1$ = 92.701	9 270.100 00
Total (per 10 000 record pairs)				10 000.000 00

characters of the full alphabetical versions agree up to a total of seven, and that the names are of equal length (i.e. no truncation of one version relative to the other within the first seven characters).

2. *Four characters agree* implies that the N Y S I I S code agrees, that the first four characters of the full alphabetical versions agree, and that there is either a disagreement or a relative truncation involving the fifth, sixth, or seventh character.

3. *N Y S I I S only agrees* implies that there is either a DISAGREEMENT or a relative truncation in the second, third, or fourth character.

4. Where the *N Y S I I S disagrees*, no comparison will be made.

Usually the NYSIIS code will have been based on up to nine characters of the full alphabetical surname, but only the first seven of these will be compared in record pairs for which the NYSIIS agrees.

Again, calculation of the outcome frequencies depends on knowledge of both the *lengths* of the names being compared, and the fortuitous *likelihoods* of AGREEMENT of various numbers of characters.

To determine how often surnames of various lengths will be compared with each other when brought together at random, a 'matrix' is constructed as before. Where we are considering lengths of up to seven characters, this will be a 7 × 7 matrix. The size of the matrix is not reduced by the smaller number of outcomes to be recognized separately; this is because the distinction between a FULL AGREEMENT and a relative truncation requires that the lengths not be pooled into groups. For example, one would not want the comparisons ADAM–ADAM or BARR–BARR to be treated in the same manner as ADAM–ADAM*S* or BARR–BARR *Y*. Both represent four-letter agreements, but in the first case there is a FULL AGREEMENT of the whole surname whereas in the second there is a relative truncation. The full 7 × 7 matrix is required in order to preserve such distinctions.

In the example chosen, the percentages of records with various numbers of characters are taken to be:

7 (41%), 6 (25%), 5 (22%), 4 (9%), 3 (2%), 2 (1%), and 1 (0%).

Again, we will assume that the two files are identical in this respect. The possible random combinations of name lengths, and their frequencies, are shown in Fig. F.6. The letters refer to the search file

File being searched

	B7 (41%)	B6 (25%)	B5 (22%)	B4 (9%)	B3 (2%)	B2 (1%)	B1 (0%)
A7 (41%)	A7,B7 (16.81%)	A7,B6 (10.25%)	A7,B5 (9.02%)	A7,B4 (3.69%)	A7,B3 (0.82%)	A7,B2 (0.41%)	A7,B1 (0.00%)
A6 (25%)	A6,B7 (10.25%)	A6,B6 (6.25%)	A6,B5 (5.50%)	A6,B4 (2.25%)	A6,B3 (0.50%)	A6,B2 (0.25%)	A6,B1 (0.00%)
A5 (22%)	A5,B7 (9.02%)	A5,B6 (5.50%)	A5,B5 (4.84%)	A5,B4 (1.98%)	A5,B3 (0.44%)	A5,B2 (0.22%)	A5,B1 (0.00%)
A4 (9%)	A4,B7 (3.69%)	A4,B6 (2.25%)	A4,B5 (1.98%)	A4,B4 (0.81%)	A4,B3 (0.18%)	A4,B2 (0.09%)	A4,B1 (0.00%)
A3 (2%)	A3,B7 (0.82%)	A3,B6 (0.50%)	A3,B5 (0.44%)	A3,B4 (0.18%)	A3,B3 (0.04%)	A3,B2 (0.02%)	A3,B1 (0.00%)
A2 (1%)	A2,B7 (0.41%)	A2,B6 (0.25%)	A2,B5 (0.22%)	A2,B4 (0.09%)	A2,B3 (0.02%)	A2,B2 (0.01%)	A2,B1 (0.00%)
A1 (0%)	A1,B7 (0.00%)	A1,B6 (0.00%)	A1,B5 (0.00%)	A1,B4 (0.00%)	A1,B3 (0.00%)	A1,B2 (0.00%)	A1,B1 (0.00%)

Search File A

Fig. F.6 Random combinations of surnames of different lengths

(A), and the file being searched (B); the numbers (7 to 1) indicate the number of letters in the surname from the particular file.

Record pairs falling in the various cells of the matrix shown in Fig. F.6 differ from cell to cell with respect to the comparison outcomes that are possible. For example, FULL AGREEMENT of a name on a record pair is possible *only* where the number of letters is the same; such pairs are represented in the cells of the diagonal A7, B7 to A1, B1. Conversely, a relative *truncation* is *not* possible in these record pairs; it may only occur where there is a difference in name length and all of the characters of the shorter version agree. There are other constraints: for example, the number of characters agreeing cannot exceed the number in the name with the fewer characters; also, the agreement portion of a mixed AGREEMENT plus DISAGREEMENT must have at least one less character than the name with the fewer characters. So, for each cell in the matrix there is a defined set of possible outcomes.

Given the probability of a fortuitous agreement (or non-agreement) of a specified number of characters at the beginning of the name, the 'general' (i.e. value non-specific) frequency of such agreements in unlinkable pairs may be applied. (The 'general' frequency pertains solely to the agreement portion of the name, and should not be confused with the 'global' frequency which takes into account any partial disagreement or truncation as well.)

For our example we will use the following general frequencies: NYSIIS + seven characters agree (0.0438%), NYSIIS + four characters agree (0.0486%), and NYSIIS only agrees (0.0876%). Intermediate levels of agreement are here taken to have the same general frequencies as do the lower levels. To avoid confusion, however, the general frequencies to be used will be explicitly stated for all levels of agreement as was done earlier for the given names:

No. of characters agreeing (N = NYSIIS)	General frequency (%)		Differences (%)		
$N+7$ or more	$p^7 =$	0.0438	$N+7$ only	$p^7 \quad =$	0.0438
$N+6$ or more	$p^6 =$	(0.0486)	$N+6$ only	$p^6 - p^7 =$	0.0048
$N+5$ or more	$p^5 =$	(0.0486)	$N+5$ only	$p^5 - p^6 =$	(0.0000)
$N+4$ or more	$p^4 =$	0.0486	$N+4$ only	$p^4 - p^5 =$	(0.0000)
$N+3$ or more	$p^3 =$	(0.0871)	$N+3$ only	$p^3 - p^4 =$	0.0385
$N+2$ or more	$p^2 =$	(0.0871)	$N+2$ only	$p^2 - p^3 =$	(0.0000)
$N+1$ or more	$p^1 =$	(0.0871)	$N+1$ only	$p^1 - p^2 =$	(0.0000)
$N+0$ or more	$p^N =$	0.0871	$N+0$ only	$p^N - p^1 =$	(0.0000)
$0+0$ or more	$p^0 =$	100.0000	$0+0$ only	$p^0 - p^N =$	99.9129

Assignment of the numbers shown within parentheses in the Table may seem arbitrary, but it is not. Where this is done correctly, the outcome frequencies calculated for the cells of the matrix should add up to 100 per cent; but if the numbers in parentheses are wrongly assigned, that is unlikely to be the case.

When using these frequencies for the actual calculation, the contents of the matrix are best rearranged as described earlier (p. 167) (see Table F.6).

Before the examples of the probabilities are filled in to make a usable table, a further rearrangement is needed to group the outcomes into three categories — FULL AGREEMENT, AGREEMENT plus truncation, and AGREEMENT plus DISAGREEMENT. Within these groupings the outcomes will be

Table F.5 Calculated frequencies of agreements, partial agreements, and disagreements of given names in randomly paired records (example)

Comparison outcomes (maximum of 7 characters)	Percentage frequencies (example)		
	of name length combinations in which these can occur	of these outcomes among all record pairs	of these outcomes where the initial already agrees
FULL AGREEMENT			
2–7 agree	20.72	0.263	3.60
AGREEMENT plus truncation			
4–6 agree + blank	45.70	0.573	7.85
3 agree + blank	31.60	0.464	6.36
2 2 agree + blank	1.98	0.052	0.71
AGREEMENT plus DISAGREEMENT			
4–6 agree + disagree	45.74	0.026	0.36
3 agree + disagree	62.41	0.114	1.56
2 agree + disagree	98.01	1.143	15.66
1 agree + disagree	100.00	4.664	63.90
DISAGREEMENT			
0 agree + disagree	100.00	92.701	0.00
Total (per cent)		100.000	100.00

arranged in descending order of the size of the agreement portion of the surname. Here, the percentages represented by the three categories of outcome will add up to more than 100. This is because, for most of the comparison pairs, there will be more than one possible level of agreement as indicated in Table F.6. The further rearrangement is shown in Table F.7.

As before, this kind of table is usable but unnecessarily large for the purpose of calculating FREQUENCY RATIOS. There is no special reason to have the FULL AGREEMENTS broken down by the size of the agreement portion of the surname. For the other two

Table F.6 Matrix information (Fig. F.6) rearranged in order of the number of letters of the surname that can be compared (N = NYSIIS code)

Nos. of characters in the two names	% of all pairs (example from Fig. F.6)	cumulative	Probabilities of various numbers of letters agreeing								
			$N+7$	$N+6$	$N+5$	$N+4$	$N+3$	$N+2$	$N+1$	$N+0$	$0+0$
7, 7	1.21	1.21	p_7^*	p_6-p_7	p_5-p_6	p_4-p_5	p_3-p_4	p_2-p_3	p_1-p_2	p_N-p_1	p_0-p_N
6, 6	4.84		—	p_6^*	p_5-p_6	p_4-p_5	p_3-p_4	p_2-p_3	p_1-p_2	p_N-p_1	p_0-p_N
6, 7	4.84	10.89	—	p_6^{**}	p_5-p_6	p_4-p_5	p_3-p_4	p_2-p_3	p_1-p_2	p_N-p_1	p_0-p_N
5, 5	6.25		—	—	p_5^*	p_4-p_5	p_3-p_4	p_2-p_3	p_1-p_2	p_N-p_1	p_0-p_N
5, 6+	16.50	33.64	—	—	p_5^{**}	p_4-p_5	p_3-p_4	p_2-p_3	p_1-p_2	p_N-p_1	p_0-p_N
4, 4	4.41		—	—	—	p_4^*	p_3-p_4	p_2-p_3	p_1-p_2	p_N-p_1	p_0-p_N
4, 5+	24.36	62.41	—	—	—	p_4^{**}	p_3-p_4	p_2-p_3	p_1-p_2	p_N-p_1	p_0-p_N
3, 3	4.00		—	—	—	—	p_3^*	p_2-p_3	p_1-p_2	p_N-p_1	p_0-p_N
3, 4+	31.60	98.01	—	—	—	—	p_3^{**}	p_2-p_3	p_1-p_2	p_N-p_1	p_0-p_N
2, 2	0.01		—	—	—	—	—	p_2^*	p_1-p_2	p_N-p_1	p_0-p_N
2, 3+	1.98	100.00	—	—	—	—	—	p_2^{**}	p_1-p_2	p_N-p_1	p_0-p_N
1, 1	0.00		—	—	—	—	—	—	p_1^*	p_N-p_1	p_0-p_N
1, 2+	0.00	100.00	—	—	—	—	—	—	p_1^{**}	p_N-p_1	p_0-p_N

*Full agreements are possible with these, but not with the others.
**Relative truncations are possible with these, but not with the others.

Table F.7 Matrix information (Fig. F.6) rearranged again, by category of outcome, and in descending order of the size of the agreement portion of the surname (N = NYSIIS code)

Size of agreement portion	Nos. of characters available on the two records	% of the record pairs involved (example) (C)	% probability of that level of agreement (example) (P)	Combined probability per 10 000 among all record pairs (C × P)
Exact AGREEMENT				
$N+7$	7, 7	16.81	$p^7 = 0.0438$	0.736 278
$N+6$	6, 6	6.25	$p^6 = 0.0486$	0.303 750
$N+5$	5, 5	4.84	$p^5 = 0.0486$	0.235 224
$N+4$	4, 4	0.81	$p^4 = 0.0486$	0.039 366
$N+3$	3, 3	0.04	$p^3 = 0.0871$	0.003 484
$N+2$	2, 2	0.01	$p^2 = 0.0871$	0.000 871
$N+1$	1, 1	0.00	$p^1 = 0.0871$	0.000 000
AGREEMENT plus truncation				
$N+6$	6, 7	20.50	$p^6 = 0.0486$	0.996 300
$N+5$	5, 6+	29.04	$p^5 = 0.0486$	1.411 344
$N+4$	4, 5+	15.84	$p^4 = 0.0486$	0.769 824
$N+3$	3, 4+	3.88	$p^3 = 0.0871$	0.337 948
$N+2$	2, 3+	1.98	$p^2 = 0.0871$	0.172 458
$N+1$	1, 2+	0.00	$p^1 = 0.0871$	0.000 000
AGREEMENT plus DISAGREEMENT				
$N+6$	7, 7	16.81	$p^6 - p^7 = 0.0048$	0.080 688
$N+5$	6+, 6+	43.56	$p^5 - p^6 = 0.0000$	0.000 000
$N+4$	5+, 5+	77.44	$p^4 - p^5 = 0.0000$	0.000 000
$N+3$	4+, 4+	94.09	$p^3 - p^4 = 0.0385$	3.622 465
$N+2$	3+, 3+	98.01	$p^2 - p^3 = 0.0000$	0.000 000
$N+1$	2+, 2+	100.00	$p^1 - p^2 = 0.0000$	0.000 000
$N+0$	1+, 1+	100.00	$p^N - p^1 = 0.0000$	0.000 000
$0+0$	1+, 1+	100.00	$p^0 - p^N = 99.9129$	9.991.290 000
Total (per 10 000 record pairs)				10 000.000 000

Table F.8 Calculated frequencies of agreements, partial agreements, and disagreements of surnames in randomly paired records (example)

Comparison outcomes (NYSIIS plus maximum of 7 characters compared)	Percentage frequencies (example)		
	of name length combinations in which these can occur	of these outcomes among all record pairs	of these outcomes where the NYSIIS already agrees
FULL AGREEMENT			
NYSIIS + 2–7 agree	28.76	0.013 190	15.14
PARTIAL AGREEMENT (with truncation or disagreement)			
NYSIIS + 4–6 agree	—	0.032 581	37.41
NYSIIS + 0–3 agree	100.00	0.041 329	47.45
DISAGREEMENT			
NYSIIS disagrees	100.00	99.912 900	0.00
Total (per cent)		100.000 000	100.00

categories, agreements of four, five and six characters are treated as carrying identical discriminating powers and are combined. Also, since the NYSIIS code has already been used for blocking, there will be no comparisons where it disagrees. Table F.8 contains the resulting condensed version of the necessary information.

Calculations of this kind are too time consuming to be repeated routinely. However, there is an advantage in having done the calculation at least once, because this permits close examination of the logical options for the comparison rules. For example, one can see more readily that a pooling of all agreements of the NYSIIS plus four letters would be unnecessarily crude. This is because full agreement of a surname consisting of four letters ought not to be confused with partial agreement in which the four agreement letters are followed by a relative truncation or a disagreement.

In routine practice, it would be preferable to obtain the DENOMINATORS for the relevant FREQUENCY RATIOS directly from an appropriate real file of UNLINKABLE pairs of records.

Appendix G:

Constructing a file of randomly matched unlinkable pairs

Considerable experience has been gained at Statistics Canada in recent years, in the routine construction of an appropriate comparison file of UNLINKABLE pairs of records for each new linkage job. The important features of such a procedure are:

(1) that it ensure the records are *randomly paired*;
(2) that the process be *convenient* and *simple*.

Beyond this,

(3) the *size* of the file of UNLINKABLE pairs should be adequate;
(4) the *contamination* with LINKABLE pairs should be low;
(5) the paired records should represent *unbiased samples* from the files to be linked.

There are various ways of ensuring that records from the search file and those from the file being searched will be *paired at random* and will be UNLINKABLE. One way would involve the use of random numbers assigned by the computer to the individual records. The steps might be as follows:

1. *Assign* a different *random number* to each record in the search file, and to each record in the file being searched.
2. *Sort* each file into numerical sequence by these numbers.
3. *Renumber* the records of the two files serially, starting with the number 'one' in both files.
4. *Match* by this new serial number the records of the search file with those of the file being searched.
5. *Exclude* any record pairs in which the NYSIIS codes and the DATES OF BIRTH both agree; each of these search records will, however, be provided with an alternative partner from the file being searched.

This would create one randomly matched pair for every record in the search file, assuming it is the smaller of the two files. The procedure also greatly reduces any contamination with fortuitous correct links.
Where the search file is smaller than one wishes the file of

UNLINKABLE pairs to be, the procedure would be modified to permit each search record to pair with a predetermined number of records from the file being searched. Suppose, for example, that each search record is to be paired separately with 10 different records from that file. The records in the search file would still be renumbered serially as described in Step 3 above. But records from the file being searched would be grouped by tens (plus perhaps a few extras with which to replace any pairings rejected because of NYSIIS plus DATE OF BIRTH agreements). Within each such group all records would receive the same serial number in Step 3. Thus, there would be 10 records with serial number 1 that would be permitted to form pairs with search record number 1, 10 with serial number 2 that would be permitted to form pairs with search record number 2, and so on. This way, a search file of 500 records would generate a file of 5000 UNLINKABLE pairs; by changing the group size to 100+ they could generate a file of 50 000 UNLINKABLE pairs, and so on.

The *size* of the file of UNLINKABLE pairs would depend in part on what is convenient. It is not difficult to create a file of 50 000 such pairs, and this would be sufficiently large to provide global frequencies for most of the rare outcomes. Much smaller files of this kind, containing 1000 or so pairs, would be less useful but are better than none at all. Much larger files of the same sort would permit measurement of the frequencies of some of the rare value-specific outcomes, but this should only be necessary where there is doubt concerning the conversions from the global outcome frequencies to their value-specific counterparts.

Such randomly matched pairs would be largely free of *contamination* with unwanted LINKABLE pairs, due to the exclusion of any pairs in which the NYSIIS codes and the DATES OF BIRTH both agree. Further reduction of such contamination is unlikely to be needed, but is possible. For example, rejections could be based on the NYSIIS agreements alone, or the DATE OF BIRTH AGREEMENTS alone, provided outcome frequencies were not derived for the identifier so used, because these would be biased by the exclusions. Such bias is minimal with the proposed scheme, which has the advantage of not requiring the creation of two separate files of randomly matched pairs.

Where the file being searched is very large there will be the further problem of how best to obtain a *random sample* from it. In the case of a file of death records, use could be made of the serial numbers (i.e. death registration numbers) that are assigned routinely at source. This existing number would permit selection of a systematic sample consisting of every 10th, or every 100th, or every 1000th record, regardless of the order in which the death records are maintained. Such a sample would be essentially random with respect to the contents of the records.

Once the rules for constructing an appropriate file of UNLINKABLE pairs have been chosen, the next most important consideration is the establishment of a convenient routine by which such files are created afresh each time a new linkage job is started.

Appendix H:

Details of phonetic coding systems for names

Phonetic coding systems are employed most frequently to bring together variant spellings of what are essentially the same names. For this purpose, the files may be sequenced by the code, and the comparisons are then carried out only between records having the same codes. Occasionally, phonetic coding is used instead to reveal similarities between names even where the codes themselves may differ. A third use of such codes, simply to reduce the sizes of the names, is rare.

Only the most commonly employed phonetic coding systems are discussed here. Most such systems have two features in common:

1. The vowel information is either partially or wholly suppressed because of its instability.
2. Certain consonants with similar sounds (or groups of letters containing these consonants) are replaced by a standard character (or group of characters) representing that sound.

Both the NYSIIS and the Soundex codes possess these features. However, the NYSIIS retains information on the sequence of vowels in the name by changing them all to the letter 'A', whereas the Soundex gets rid of the vowels. 'Name compression' and the 'ill-spelled name routine' resemble the Soundex in this respect.

All of the above codes are capable of revealing similarities between names even where the coded forms do not agree precisely. However, only the ill-spelled name routine has been systematically applied to distinguish different degrees of similarity where comparisons between names are carried out freely.

Finally, where shortened forms of the names are needed for compactness, name compression may be desirable because it loses only the vowels and the redundant consonants.

Details of the rules for such codings are now given.

H.1. The NYSIIS code

The NYSIIS coding proceeds in well-defined steps. The first letter(s) of a name are tested and changed as necessary. The same is done for the last letter(s) of the name. Then, starting with the second letter a scan is carried out of each letter of the name using an imaginary 'pointer' and, at each step, changes may be made to the name according to a set of rules called a 'loop'. The rules are applied anew each time the 'pointer' is moved to the next letter of the name. During the process, characters may be taken from the altered name and transferred to create the NYSIIS code. Finally, the end portion of the NYSIIS code as formed in this manner is subjected to a further test and changed as necessary.

Usually the NYSIIS code for a surname is based on a maximum of nine letters of the full alphabetical name, and the NYSIIS code itself is then limited to six letters. The detailed rules are:

1. *Change the first letter(s) of the name.* If xx replace with yy as follows: (a) MAC → MCC; (b) KN → NN; (c) K → C; (d) PH → FF; (d) PF → FF.

2. *Change the last letter(s) of the name.* If xx replace with yy as follows: (a) S → delete; (b) Z → delete; (c) EE → Y; (d) IE → Y; (e) DT → D; (f) RT → D; (g) RD → D.

3. *The first character of the NYSIIS code* = the first letter of the name.

4. *Set the 'pointer' to the second letter of the name.*

5. *Change the current letter(s) of the name*, i.e. at the present position of the 'pointer'. If xx replace with yy; execute one only of the following, in the order given:
(a) blank → go to rule 7; (b) EV → AF; (c) vowel (AEIOU) → A; (d) Q → G; (e) Z → S; (f) M →N; (g) KN → N; (h) K → C; (i) SCH → SSS; (j) PH → FF; (k) H preceded by or followed by a letter that is *not* a vowel (AEIOU) → replace the current position in the name with the preceding letter; (l) W preceded by a vowel → replace the current position in the name with the preceding letter; (m) if none of these rules applies; then retain the current position letter in the name.

6. If the current position letter in the name is equal to the last character placed in the NYSIIS code, do not enter it into the code. Instead, set the 'pointer' to the next letter of the name, and go to Step 5.

   The next character of the NYSIIS code = the current position letter in the name after completing Step 5 (but omitting a letter that is equal to the last character already placed in the code).

   After putting a character into the code, move the pointer forward to the next letter of the name. Then go to Step 5.

7. *Change the last character(s) of the N Y S I I S code.* If xx replace with yy as follows:
(a) S → delete; (b) AY → Y; (c) A → delete.

There is also a *modified N Y S I I S name-coding procedure* which follows the above pattern but includes additional rules. These are summarized under the numbers and headings used above, as continuations of the lists of codings already given.

1. *Change the first letter(s) of the name.* If xx replace with yy as follows:
(e) WR → RR; (f) RH → RR; (g) DG → GG; (h) vowels (AEIOU) → A.
2. *Change the last letter(s) of the name.* If xx replace with yy as follows:
(aa) drop terminal S or Z from all names before coding begins; (h) YE → Y; (i) NP → N; (j) ND → N; (k) IX → IC; (l) EX → EC; (m) JR → blank; (n) SR → blank.
5. *Change the current letter(s) of the name,* i.e. at the present position of the 'pointer'. If xx replace with yy as follows:
(ca) Y when not the last letter of the name → A; (n) SCH at end of the name → SSA; (o) SCH not at end of the name → SSS; (p) SH at end of the name → SA; (q) SH not at end of the name → SS; (r) GHT → TTT; (s) DG → GG; (t) WR → RR.
8. *Change the first character of the N Y S I I S code.* If xx replace with yy as follows:
(a) A → first letter of the original name; (b) space → first letter of the original name.

These modifications to the original N Y S I I S code are designed to deal with rare difficult cases. Thus, most names will have identical codes whichever version of the coding procedure is used.

Examples:

ANDERSEN, ANDERSON	→	ANDAR
BRIAN, BROWN, BRUN	→	BRAN
CAPP, COPE, COPP, KIPP	→	CAP
DANE, DEAN, DENT, DIONNE	→	DAN
SMITH, SCHMIT, SCHMIDT	→	SNAT
TRUEMAN, TRUMAN	→	TRANAN

H.2. The Soundex code

The Soundex code sets aside more of the unreliable components of a name than does the NYSIIS, but it also loses more of the available discriminating power in the process. This is partly because it discards information on the positions of the vowels in the name.

The steps in the coding procedure are simpler than for the NYSIIS. The first letter of the name is retained, vowels are removed, consonants are assigned numbers from 1 to 6 to represent their sounds, and redundant code numbers are removed. The detailed rules are:

1. The first letter of the name is used in its uncoded form to serve as the prefix character of the code. (The rest of the code is numerical.)
2. Thereafter, W and H are ignored entirely.
3. A, E, I, O, U, Y are not assigned a code number, but do serve as 'separators' (see Step 5).
4. Other letters of the name are converted to a numerical equivalent:

B, P, F, V	→ 1
D, T	→ 3
L	→ 4
M, N	→ 5
R	→ 6

All other consonants
(C, G, J, K, Q, S, X, Z)   → 2.

5. There are two exceptions: (a) letters that follow prefix letters which would, if coded, have the same numerical code, are ignored in all cases unless a 'separator' (see Step 3) precedes them. (b) The second letter of any pair of consonants having the same code number is likewise ignored, i.e. unless there is a 'separator' between them in the name.
6. The final Soundex code consists of the prefix letter plus three numerical characters. Longer codes are truncated to this length, and shorter codes are extended to it by adding zeros.

Examples:

ANDERSON, ANDERSEN	→	A 536
BERGMANS, BRIGHAM	→	B 625
BIRK, BERQUE, BIRCK	→	B 620
FISHER, FISCHER	→	F 260
LAVOIE, LEVOY	→	L 100
LLWELLYN	→	L 450.

H.3. Name compression and the ill-spelled name routine

'Name compression' is a way of reducing the length of a name; in addition, it serves as a preliminary step in the 'ill-spelled name routine'. For this latter reason the two are considered together.

Name compression

The rules are:

1. Delete the second of any pair of identical consonants.
2. Delete A, E, I, O, U, Y, except when the first letter of the name.

Examples:
    BENNETT   →   BNT
    FISHER   →   FSHR.

Ill-spelled name routine

This routine was designed to avoid a limitation inherent in other systems of coding and comparing names. With the way in which the NYSIIS and Soundex codes are commonly used, detailed comparison of the full alphabetical versions of a name is dependent on exact agreement of the phonetic codes; other degrees of similarity of the codes are not taken into account. This is true even where the codes differ with respect to just the simple insertion or deletion of a single character in the one as compared with the other.

An 'insertion' into, or a 'deletion' from, any sequenced string of characters results in what is called a 'frame shift' relative to the previous sequence. This will affect the comparison of the one version with respect to the other. If the part of the sequence on one side of the insertion/deletion point is seen to be in perfect agreement, the other part may appear totally different, and vice versa. It is all a matter of where one starts reading. The main problem is to design a comparison system that will detect similarities in spite of such frame shifts. A secondary problem is to make the system work even where there is a different insertion into each of the two sequences. The ill-spelled name routine is intended to solve both of these.

The rules are:

1. Use the name compression procedure, up to a total of four letters.
2. When comparing two such four-letter codes, search for and count the numbers of letters or blanks, up to a total of four in all, that agree without altering their sequence (i.e. skip over any inserted letters that would otherwise interrupt the sequence that agrees).
3. Any of five levels of similarity/dissimilarity may be revealed by such a comparison (i.e. 0, 1, 2, 3, or 4 agree). This 'score' may be used in various ways. For an automated linkage operation, the FREQUENCY RATIOS in LINKABLE versus UNLINKABLE pairs would be obtained for each of

the five levels of outcome, and used in calculating the ODDS in favour of a correct link. For the purposes of manual resolution, a score of 3 or 4 might indicate a need for visual comparison of the full alphabetical versions of the names.

Examples:

		Score
BOWMAN	→ *BMN*–	
BAUMAN	→ *BMN*–	4 (BMN–)
McGONE	→ *MCGN*	
McKONE	→ *MCKN*	3 (MCN)
ANGRIEFF	→ A*NGR*	
SINGER	→ S*NGR*	3 (NGR)
MCGINESS	→ *MCGN*	
MAGINNES	→ *MGN*S	3 (MGN)
LU	→ L–––	
ROO	→ R–––	3 (–––)

H.4. Special uses

Much thought has been given to the uses of phonetic name codes that are intended to agree precisely in spite of spelling differences. But the same cannot be said for the use of phonetic codes to reveal degrees of similarity and dissimilarity. In fact, the ill-spelled name routine has set something of a precedent, and the concept is worthy of further exploration. One possible application is in the simultaneous comparison and cross-comparison of first and second given names.

A procedure was described earlier (p. 45) for obtaining the relevant FREQUENCY RATIOS for the different outcome levels from a simultaneous comparison and cross-comparison of the first and second initials. The procedure was not extended to include whole given names because of the added complexity, especially where some are represented only by initials or are absent altogether. However, where both given names are present in full on a pair of records, it might indeed be useful to compare and cross-compare them simultaneously.

In the past, comparisons of the full given names have only taken place where the initials already agreed. This restriction was adopted with reluctance because of the resulting losses of potential discriminating power, as with the names CARL versus KARL. The reason for its adoption was that it greatly simplifies calculation of the FREQUENCY RATIOS. An alternative procedure might be workable, however. For example, a more permissive rule would be to compare (and cross-compare) the full alphabetical names only where the ill-spelled name routine indicated a 'score' of 3 or 4. The disadvantage is that this would further complicate calculation of appropriate FREQUENCY RATIOS by adding to the large number of multiple levels of outcome already being recognized. However, a compromise comparison scheme might be devised that would make the approach both workable and sound.

The reason for raising this possibility is that the idea of using a phonetic code to quantify the degree of similarity of names has not so far been adequately explored, either conceptually or empirically.

Appendix I:

Design of a computer linkage system

For one-time users of computerized record linkage, *ad hoc* programs that incorporate their particular rules may be reasonably simple to write and use. However, where a succession of diverse linkage jobs has to be carried out, this approach will become unnecessarily laborious and time consuming. It is better to have a generalized computer system that will ensure flexibility of the linkage procedures with a minimum of subsequent programming. As well, a computer system may be designed to assist with virtually all aspects of each linkage operation from start to finish. A system of this kind, known as 'GIRLS' ('Generalized Iterative Record Linkage System') or CANLINK, has been developed at Statistics Canada and used routinely, there and at other centres, since the early 1980s.

The main features of any such a system relate to:

(1) the *input* to the computer, including the *files* to be linked and the *rules* to be employed;

(2) the *linkage* proper as carried out within the computer, including the *comparison* steps and the *eliminations* of unsuccessful candidate pairs of records; and

(3) the *output* from the computer, including *reports* on the linkage status of the record pairs, and a feedback of *information* on the discriminating powers of the comparison outcomes (i.e. the frequency ratios, for LINKED versus UNLINKABLE pairs of records) as defined by the rules used for the linkages, and perhaps also by alternative rules that might have been used instead.

Readers requiring design details beyond those in the present overview are referred to the documentation for the existing system at Statistics Canada (Hill 1981; Hill and Pring-Mill 1985, 1986). The reader is also referred to a published description of GIRLS by Howe and Lindsay (1981).

The following sections are not intended to describe a particular computer system. However, there will inevitably be strong resemblances to the approach used in GIRLS. This is because of the all-embracing nature of that system and the fact that it has been so well documented.

I.1. Input to the computer

Before the computer can begin a linkage operation it needs access to:

(1) the *files* that are to be linked to each other;
(2) the names and definitions of the *identifier fields* to be compared;
(3) the *prior probability* that a search record will match correctly on a single try, with a randomly selected record from the file being searched;
(4) the DISCRIMINATING POWERS of the identifiers and of the outcomes from comparisons between them; and
(5) *rules* that say what comparisons to make, how to distinguish and eliminate records pairs which are unlikely to be correctly matched, and how to establish group of records where more than two may be correctly linked to each other.

The files to be linked — preprocessing

For the computer to be able to make use of the files that are to be linked, the formats of the records and of the identifiers need to be standardized, sequencing or blocking information has to be assigned, and the files require sorting into an appropriate sequence for searching. During this *preprocessing*, rules are applied to ensure uniformity, especially with respect to the names.

1. There will be an edit to detect inappropriate characters and correct them wherever possible.
2. Unwanted titles will be deleted (M R, M R S, J R).
3. Punctuation marks and blank spaces are either standardized or removed (O'CONNOR, MC KAY, ST JOHN).

In addition, existing codes may be checked and new codes assigned (e.g. for marital status, sex, place of birth), duplicate entry records pertaining to the same 'event' will be created where a given identifier has been reported in more than one way on the same record, and records for the two sexes may be put into separate files.

Defining the identifier fields

The identifier fields need to be assigned names that the computer will recognize (e.g. SURNAME, GIVEN1, GIVEN2, INIT1, INIT2, BIRTHYR, BIRTHMO, BIRTHDY). These are used when writing instructions for the comparison procedures. Where an identifier field is employed in more than one way it may be assigned more than one name, as when initials are compared first and the remainders of the given names later. Fields may also be described for the computer in terms of the numbers of characters they contain, the nature of those characters (e.g. alphanumerical, numerical, binary), and the number of possible field values. This will indicate how the information is to be handled.

Deriving prior probabilities

The ABSOLUTE ODDS in favour of a correct linkage, and its logarithm the ABSOLUTE TOTAL WEIGHT, have two components. In part, these are determined by the *prior probability* that a search record will find a correctly matching record in a single random draw from the file that is being searched. And in part, they reflect the RELATIVE ODDS or RELATIVE TOTAL WEIGHT derived from the combined frequency ratios for the observed outcomes from all the identifier comparisons.

This prior probability of a correct match on first try also has two components: first, the probability that a correct match for the particular search record exists in the file being searched, and second, the number of records in that file. The overall prior probability is equal to the first of these divided by the second. The logarithms of both may be treated as weights, and both weights will be negative; in other words, neither logarithm can be greater than zero. Together they represent the 'hurdle' that the discriminating power of the identifiers will have to surmount if there is to be a linkage. These serve to convert the RELATIVE ODDS based on the identifiers alone into the ABSOLUTE ODDS in favour of a correct link.

The probability that a search record has a correct match in the file being searched may be obtained in either of two ways. A preliminary linkage will yield a reasonably accurate average probability. Alternatively, in the case of a death search life tables can predict for an individual the probability that his or her death will have occurred in the period covered by the death file, or in a specified part of that period (usually the year of deaths represented by the death record with which a search record is being compared).

Deriving discriminating powers

The DISCRIMINATING POWERS of the identifiers and of the outcomes from their comparisons have also to be determined and fed to the computer. The data come in part from the file of *unpaired* records that is being searched, and in part from the LINKED pairs of records (initially those created by a preliminary linkage) together with a comparison file of randomly matched unlinkable pairs.

From the *unpaired* records that are being searched are derived the frequencies of the various values of identifiers such as surnames, initials, given names, places of birth. The logarithms of these frequencies are called 'FREQUENCY WEIGHTS'. They represent the probabilities of fortuitous full agreements of the particular values. A weighted mean of the frequencies, derived at the same time for each such identifier, is the basis of a 'GENERAL FREQUENCY' or GENERAL WEIGHT. A general frequency or weight represents the likelihood of fortuitous full agreement of that identifier regardless of the particular value.

When the general weight is subtracted from the frequency weight for a particular value, the difference is termed an ADJUSTMENT WEIGHT. This difference represents the degree to which that value of the identifier has a higher or lower DISCRIMINATING POWER than an average or 'representative' value. ADJUSTMENT WEIGHTS are best stored in look-up tables because there are as many of them as there are values of the identifiers. Surnames and given names are treated in this manner, along with truncated versions of these; so also are the places of birth. It must be emphasized that such frequency weights and their derivatives are all based on *unpaired* records; they therefore differ in kind from the weights based on *pairs* of records, that is, on the identifier comparison outcome frequencies in files of *paired* records.

From the LINKED pairs of records (e.g. produced by a preliminary linkage), and from a comparison file of UNLINKED pairs, are obtained the frequencies of the various levels of outcome (e.g. full agreement, different degrees of similarity and dissimilarity, and more extreme disagreement; or the combinations of values as when place of work is compared with place of death). The logarithms of these outcome frequencies are called 'GLOBAL WEIGHTS' or, to be more precise, components of the global weights. Those based on the outcomes in linked pairs are *negative components* of the global weights, and those from the outcomes in unlinked pairs are *positive components*. The sum of a negative and a positive component is a NET GLOBAL WEIGHT. In the absence of an actual file of unlinked pairs the positive components can, in principle, be calculated instead of measured. However, although some of the calculations are simple, others are tedious, time consuming, and error prone. Measured values are therefore to be preferred.

The global weights are usually (but not always) non-specific for value and so do not need to be stored in look-up tables. They are written directly into the comparison rules. The essential distinction between GLOBAL and GENERAL weights lies in their origins, and also in their uses. GLOBAL weights reflect the full definition of the particular outcome level from an identifier comparison. The distinction is of practical importance for the partial agreements, because the global weight takes account of both the *agreement* portion and the *non-agreement* portion of the outcome definition. Neither a frequency weight nor a general weight can do that because they are based on single records, not record pairs; no actual comparison is involved as in the global weights.

To convert a GLOBAL WEIGHT to its value-specific counterpart, the ADJUSTMENT WEIGHT for the particular value of the agreement portion of the identifier is added to the global weight. The adjustment may be either positive (for rare names and such) or negative (for common names and such).

When the weight for the prior probability is added to the value-specific weights for the various outcome frequencies or FREQUENCY RATIOS pertaining to a record pair, the result is an ABSOLUTE TOTAL WEIGHT representing the absolute odds in favour of a correct link.

The rules for linkage

The rules that are fed to the computer specify each step of the linkage procedure. Of all the rules, the most crucial are those governing the *identifier comparisons*, the assignment of GLOBAL WEIGHTS to the outcomes from these, and the use of ADJUSTMENT WEIGHTS to convert the global weights to their *value-specific* counterparts. These are the heart of the linkage system. Views concerning what constitute the best comparison procedures have evolved with experience. The

feedback of empirical results has indicated the need for improvements and the directions these should take.

Emphasis was at one time mainly on the simple AGREEMENT and
DISAGREEMENT outcomes. Separate recognition of the PARTIAL
AGREEMENTS was regarded as occasionally useful but not widely
needed. As the true importance of the 'PARTIALS' began to be
understood, problems emerged that limited their usefulness. The
most serious of these was the lack of a simple correct procedure for
routinely converting the GLOBAL weights for the partial agreements
to *value-specific* weights. Only recently has this problem been
solved.

Multiple levels of outcome are now readily usable; they are also
often essential for efficient exploitation of the available discriminating power. For comparisons of YEAR OF BIRTH, MONTH OF
BIRTH, and DAY OF BIRTH the degrees of agreement and disagreement are best viewed as forming a spectrum with no abrupt transition at any point. A fine breakdown of the levels of similarity and
dissimilarity is appropriate also for comparisons of SURNAMES and
GIVEN NAMES. Likewise for comparisons of PLACE OF WORK
with PLACE OF DEATH, the possible combinations of places may be
correctly regarded as ranging from highly likely to highly unlikely,
and the associated net weights clearly confirm or modify one's
subjective impressions in the matter.

Only for INITIALS, MARITAL STATUS, and PLACE OF BIRTH
is it still customary to limit the outcome levels to simple
AGREEMENT and DISAGREEMENT; but even for these the simplification results in reduced efficiency. For INITIALS it would be
better to concatenate the first with the second to permit comparison
and cross-comparison simultaneously. So-called 'disagreements'
involving the initial 'C' with the initial 'K' (as in Carl and Karl)
would be better treated as partial agreements or, to be more precise,
as representing a special 'level' of outcome. For MARITAL STATUS
much of the discriminating power resides in such unlikely combinations as 'married' followed by 'never married'. And for PLACE OF
BIRTH it would be desirable to treat such outcomes as 'Canada'
versus 'Ontario' as partial agreements.

The nature of the more flexible comparison patterns reflects
increasingly the mental processes by which difficult matches are
sometimes resolved manually. The human mind is capable of recognizing clues that would escape the computer where the comparison

rules are artificially restrictive. The working of the human mind in such matters may seem complicated, but it is also natural and understandable. Whenever a similar degree of sophistication is developed for the computer it can be employed repeatedly. The central processor is as capable of handling refined rules as crude ones, and at virtually the same cost.

I.2. Steps in the linkage proper, within the computer

The steps by which linkage is accomplished within the computer have been described in the main text (pp. 75–86) and are listed here in summary form only. These may be regarded as a series of rejection procedures. They begin by employing crude rules to eliminate the obviously unlinkable candidate pairs that are initially exceedingly numerous, and continue in stages using increasingly refined criteria as the numbers of pairs to be tested declines. The steps are:

1. *Restricting the comparison pairs.*
    (a) Compare the BLOCKING or sequencing information first (e.g. the surname NYSIIS code).
    (b) Avoid creating comparison pairs where the BLOCKING information disagrees.
2. *Preliminary rejections.*
    (a) Compare *key identifiers* only (e.g. first and second initials, year, month, and day of birth).
    (b) Reject all pairs for which there is no agreement of any *key identifier.*
3. Weighting for the *prior probability* of a correct link on a single random pairing.
    (a) Assign a negative weight for the probability that a search record has a *correctly matching* record in the file being searched. (This may be based on an average probability drawn from a preliminary linkage, or on life-table data specific for the particular search record and the year of the death record with which it is currently being compared.)
    (b) Assign a second negative weight for the *size of the file* being searched. (This may be the whole file or, in the case of a death search, the file for the particular year of deaths.)
    (N.B. The above two weights must relate to the same file, i.e. either to the whole of the file being searched, or to the same part of that file, such as a particular year of deaths.)
4. Rejecting on the basis of *value non-specific* discriminating power.
    (a) Compare the identifiers on the current record pair and assign GLOBAL weights to the outcomes.

    (b) The comparison sequence for a given pair may be aborted by an *early cut-off* as soon as it becomes evident that an acceptable total weight cannot result even if all subsequent identifiers comparisons yield an agreement outcome.

    (c) Sum the weights from Steps 3 and 4 above to get an ABSOLUTE TOTAL weight which is *value non-specific*.

    (d) Set temporary *thresholds* that are unlikely to lose good links. (These will be well below zero total weight.)

    (e) Reject on the basis of this *value non-specific* total weight.

5. Rejecting on the basis of *value-specific* discriminating power.

    (a) Add ADJUSTMENT WEIGHTS to convert the GLOBAL weights to their value-specific counterparts.

       (N.B. The FREQUENCY weights alone are *not* an adequate basis for this conversion. If used, they yield incorrect value-specific weights for the PARTIAL AGREEMENT outcomes.)

    (b) Sum the weights again to get an ABSOLUTE TOTAL weight which is now *value-specific*.

    (c) Set new thresholds. (These will be negative but closer to zero than before.)

    (d) Reject on the basis of this *value-specific* total weight.

6. Weight updating and *iteration*.

    (a) Using the linked pairs from Step 5, recalculate the *negative* components of weight.

    (b) *Update* the weights and recalculate the ABSOLUTE TOTAL WEIGHT.

    (c) Repeat (*iterate*) Step 5.

7. Grouping.

    (a) *Group* any pairs that have a record in common. (To bring more of the unlinked records into pairs and groups, lower the threshold for linkage.)

    (b) *Resolve* the conflicts created by records that link to more than one group. (To reduce the number of such conflicts, raise the threshold.)

    (c) *Optimize* the grouping (i.e. readjust the threshold to get the best balance between unlinked records and conflicting linkages. A manual override may be used where necessary.)

Special features of the above steps are:

(a) The *preliminary rejections* — these are an effective economy measure.

(b) The *prior probability* of a correct link on a single random try — the weights for this are used to convert overall RELATIVE ODDS to overall ABSOLUTE ODDS when all the weights for a record pair are summed.

(c) The ADJUSTMENT WEIGHTS — these convert the GLOBAL weights for agreements and partial agreements, to their *value-specific* counterparts. (Frequency weights by themselves are unsuitable for this purpose and cause errors when applied to partial agreements.)

(d) The WEIGHT *update* and *iteration* — these enable crude negative components of weight to be used initially and refined later.

I.3. Output from the computer

Computer systems designed to handle all aspects of a record linkage operation should be capable of assisting in many ways. One kind of assistance concerns the output of data arising from the completion of a linkage operation. Three examples of the most frequently used products from the linkages are given here:

(1) *reports* on the linkage status of record pairs;
(2) *listings* of linked pairs and groups;
(3) *information* on outcome frequencies as a basis for the global FREQUENCY RATIOS and GLOBAL WEIGHTS.

Reports on linkage status

Reports on the linkage status of particular record pairs may usefully contain considerable detail. Of special interest are the weights for the *prior probabilities* of a correct linkage on a single random pairing, the *identifiers* compared, the *outcomes* from the comparisons, the negative and positive components of the GLOBAL WEIGHTS for these outcomes, the ADJUSTMENT WEIGHTS used to convert the global weights to value-specific weights, and the ABSOLUTE TOTAL WEIGHT representing the overall ABSOLUTE ODDS in favour of a correct linkage. The reports might also contain other particulars on which weights are based, for example the calendar *years* of the two records, the *size of the file* being searched, and the *ages* of the individual at the times of the two records. These latter sorts of information provide the basis of some of the weights for the prior probabilities.

For the example in Table I.1, use is made of the outcome frequencies for *linked* pairs of records and *unlinked* pairs. These frequencies have been converted to weights (i.e. logarithms to the base 2, multiplied by 10) before being used in Table I.1.

Listings of linked pairs and groups

The kinds of information given in the full report above may be

Table I.1 Example of a report on the linkage status of a record pair

Identifiers compared	Field values		Outcome level	Global		Specific adjustment	Net weight
	Record A	Record B		Negative weight	Positive weight		
Basic data							
Record	Work	Death					
Year	1956	1981					
Age	33	59					
Weights for prior probability							
Probability of dying in 1981 (= 2.91%)							−51
Size of the 1981 death file (= 98 100)							−166
Weights for DISCRIMINATING POWERS							
NYSIIS	BRAN	BRAN					
SURNAME	BROWN	BROWN	1	−1	+54	−32	+21
INITIALS	JF	JF	1	−8	+90	−11 (J) +8 (F)	+79
GIVEN 11	JOHN	JOHN	1	−3	+28	−11	+14
GIVEN 22	FRANK	FRANK	1	−3	+28	−4	+21
GIVEN 12							
GIVEN 21							

Table I.1—*Continued*

Identifiers compared	Field values		Outcome level	Global			Specific adjustment	Net weight
	Record A	Record B		Negative weight	Positive weight			
BIRTHYR	1923	1922	2	−27	+55			+28
BIRTHMO	08	08	1	−1	+36			+35
BIRTHDY	17	17	1	−2	+49			+47
BIRTHPLZ**	PEI	PEI	1	−2	+31			+64
EVENTPL†	Timmins	Sudbury	2	−4	+15		+35	+11

Combined WEIGHTS and combined ODDS

ABSOLUTE TOTAL WEIGHT   +103

ABSOLUTE OVERALL ODDS   1261/1

*Included with the global weights may be some for which a limited amount of specificity is already built into the instructions to the computer (e.g. as with EVENTPL above).

**PEI is the small Canadian province of Prince Edward Island.

†Both Timmins and Sudbury are Ontario mining centres.

summarized in a single line for each of the two records in the matched pair. Presentation in this fashion permits the linkage information to be displayed as a *listing* of matched pairs or groups of records. The essential details for this purpose consist of the various identifier values, plus the TOTAL WEIGHT for the linkage. Pairs of lines relating to a matched pair of records (or groups of lines relating to a group of records) that are being considered for linkage to each other, may be single spaced to facilitate visual comparison of the identifiers. Between pairs or groups there would be a double space to distinguish these from each other. Converted to this form the information from Table I.1 would appear as follows:

			Sur-	Given	Given	BIRTH				
Weight	Record	Code	name	1	2	Yr	Mo	Dy	Place	Eventpl
+ 103	Work (1956)	Bran	Brown	John	Frank	1923	08	17	PEI	Timmins
	Death (1981)	Bran	Brown	John	Frank	1922	08	17	PEI	Sudbury

    Such listings are best arrayed in descending order of total weight. The pairs about which there is least doubt will then come first, while those likely to require the closest visual examination are clustered together, followed by pairs with diminishing likelihoods of being correctly linked. Because the various linkages to group members will often have different total weights, the position of a group in the sequence will be determined by the largest of the weights for a linkage to a group member.
    Visual examination of these listings provides valuable feedback. Borderline links may be examined to see whether there are clues concerning the linkage status that the computer has missed. Subjective disagreements with the calculated odds may reveal an alternative logic in the human mind; the rules for the computer might then be changed to resemble more closely those of the human. It is this kind of empirical feedback that has lead to an emphasis on multiple levels of outcome, defined as one would do in one's own head. The resulting procedures have had to be tested, but their use has imposed no special burden once the procedures had become standardized. Sophistication in record linkage is often cheaper than simplicity because it reduces subsequent clerical labour.

Information on the outcome frequencies

For each identifier that enters into a comparison, data are needed concerning the frequencies of the various levels of outcome. The global weights are drawn from such information. For each level of outcome the relevant data consist of the *counts*, the percentage *frequencies* (which may sometimes be based on a denominator that excludes comparisons represented by blank fields), and the *logarithms* of the frequencies (e.g. 10 × the log to the base 2). The latter are the GLOBAL WEIGHTS weights or, rather, the negative or positive components of these weights depending on whether the source was a file of LINKED or UNLINKABLE pairs. An example is given in Table I.2.

Where such data are derived from record pairs that are considered to be correctly linked, namely in practice those for which the errors

Table I.2 Example of information on outcome frequencies in linked and unlinkable pairs of records — year of birth differences

Outcome level			Count	Per cent	Negative weight*	Positive weight*
Outcome frequencies from LINKED pairs of records — YEAR OF BIRTH differences (with Negative Components of GLOBAL WEIGHTS)						
1 Difference =		– 0 yrs.	922	77.3	−4	
2		1 yr.	180	15.1	−27	
3	2	– 3 yrs.	46	3.9	−47	
4	4	– 6 yrs.	30	2.5	−53	
5	7	–10 yrs.	7	0.6	−74	
6	11 +	yrs.	8	0.7	−72	
Outcome frequencies from UNLINKABLE pairs of records — YEAR OF BIRTH differences (with Positive Components of GLOBAL WEIGHTS)						
1 Difference =		0 yrs.	540	1.1		+65
2		1 yr.	1 086	2.2		+55
3	2	– 3 yrs.	2 100	4.2		+46
4	4	– 6 yrs.	3 220	6.4		+40
5	7	–10 yrs.	4 423	8.9		+35
6	11 +	yrs.	38 604	77.2		+4

*The negative and positive weights are equal to 10 × $\log_2$ of the percentage frequency, and are respectively negative and positive in sign.

are small, the product will constitute a set of *negative* components of the global weights. Conversely, where they are derived from a comparison file of unlinkable, randomly matched pairs, they will constitute a corresponding set of *positive* components of the global weights.

Since the negative components will initially be based on a preliminary and imperfect file of linked pairs, they may be revised after a near-final linkage. The revision would be followed by an updating of the weights assigned to the matched pairs of records, and of the overall total weights, before final decisions are made to accept or reject.

Changing the comparison rules

As described above, the information on outcome frequencies extracted by the system would relate solely to the *comparison rules* and the *levels of outcome* actually employed in the linkage operation. These might not represent the best choices, however, and there is often a need to test alternative rules on an experimental basis. A particularly useful feature of a computer linkage system would therefore be one which permits extraction of outcome frequencies based on modified rules, without repeating the actual linkage operation.

The manner in which such a feature might be used is illustrated here in the case of comparisons of MONTH OF BIRTH. Here, there are 12 possible levels of outcome which are normally grouped arbitrarily to form a coarser breakdown when doing an actual linkage. Ideally, each such group should be internally homogeneous with respect to the NET WEIGHTS for the finer elements that have been combined in it. But one cannot be certain of the level of within-group homogeneity unless one has seen the full breakdown before deciding on the grouping, and this is not possible until after some linkages have been established. One needs to be able to see the full breakdown so as to eliminate guesswork in the matter. Table I.3 shows what this might look like, when the data are arranged so that the NET WEIGHTS can be readily calculated.

The merit in being able to view a fine breakdown of the outcome levels is that it indicates clearly which levels may appropriately be grouped and which are best left ungrouped. The usual rule of thumb when making the decision is that differences in FREQUENCY

Table I.3 Example of information on outcome frequencies in *linked* and *unlinkable* pairs* of records — full breakdown of month of birth differences

Outcome level	Difference	Frequencies Links	Frequencies Non-links (calc**)	Negative weights (from links)	Positive weights (from non-links)	Net weights
1	0 months	86.0%	12/144	− 2	+ 36	+ 34
2	1 month	7.1%	22/144	− 38	+ 27	− 11
3	2 months	3.5%	20/144	− 48	+ 28	− 20
4	3 months	1.6%	18/144	− 60	+ 30	− 30
5	4 months	0.44%	16/144	− 78	+ 32	− 46
6	5 months	0.32%	14/144	− 83	+ 34	− 49
7	6 months	0.27%	12/144	− 85	+ 36	− 49
8	7 months	0.22%	10/144	− 88	+ 38	− 50
9	8 months	0.18%	8/144	− 91	+ 42	− 49
10	9 months	0.14%	6/144	− 95	+ 46	− 49
11	10 months	0.09%	4/144	− 101	+ 52	− 49
12	11 months	0.04%	2/144	− 113	+ 62	− 51

*The frequencies and weights for a given outcome among the linked and unlinkable pairs are given here in the same line to facilitate calculation of the net weights. This will not necessarily be the form in which the computer would present the data. For the unlinkable pairs, calculated theoretical frequencies are given here, although actual measured frequencies would often be used instead.
**The calculated theoretical frequencies for the various outcomes in the non-linked pairs are given as fractions because these are more precise than the percentages.

RATIOS of twofold or more are best not pooled. Where the corresponding weights are logarithms to the base 2, multiplied by 10, this means that levels with differences in net weights of 10 or more are best not pooled. According to this rule, outcome levels 1–4 in Table I.3 should be kept separate, and levels 5–12 may be grouped into a single level. The objective is to use the available discriminating power efficiently, and to this end one does not create groups of outcome levels that are exceedingly heterogeneous with respect to their FREQUENCY RATIOS or NET WEIGHTS. Without the above mentioned fine breakdown, any groupings of outcome levels would have had to be based on guesswork.

When the grouping of outcome levels has been done according to the above rule, the data appear as shown in Table I.4. Had any of the

Table I.4 Example of information on outcome frequencies in linked and unlinkable pairs of records — grouping levels of month of birth differences that have similar net weights (the same data are used here as in Table I.3)

Outcome level	Difference	Frequencies Links	Frequencies Non-links (calc**)	Negative weights (from links)	Positive weights (from non-links)	Net weights
1	0 months	86.0%	12/144	− 2	+ 36	+ 34
2	1 month	7.1%	22/144	− 38	+ 27	− 11
3	2 months	3.5%	20/144	− 48	+ 28	− 20
4	3 months	1.6%	18/144	− 60	+ 30	− 30
5	4–11 months	1.8%	72/144	− 58	+ 10	− 48

levels of outcome in the Table been pooled when carrying out the original linkage operation, discriminating power would have been wasted. One would not be aware of this, however, had no subsequent fine breakdown been carried out as in Table I.3.

The principle is generally applicable. The pooling of any outcomes that separately have widely different FREQUENCY RATIOS or NET WEIGHTS, wastes discriminating power. When designing a comparison procedure for a given identifier, one may have no advance knowledge concerning the outcome levels or values it is appropriate to combine. Such information may only be obtained after a linked file has been established. For some identifiers one might perhaps make use of a preliminary linkage with very fine breakdowns to determine what groupings would be appropriate. But this would not be feasible, say, for comparisons of PLACE OF WORK versus PLACE OF DEATH; even where the search records pertained to a single place of work there would probably be a long list of actual places of death. A more generally applicable alternative is to extract, where needed, the frequencies of all possible outcome levels or values after a linked file has already been established. Based on this information, decisions would be made concerning the most appropriate groupings of outcomes.

The aim is to optimize the use of discriminating power, and to remove guesswork from decisions on how best to group or break down the levels of outcome from a given identifier comparison. The results would consist of revised sets of comparison procedures, outcomes, and their weights. These might be applied, either in an iteration of the linkage step, or as just a recalculation of the total weights for existing record pairs.

Other linkage reports and information from the computer

No attempt will be made to list the numerous other kinds of linkage reports and data pertaining to a linkage operation that may usefully be obtained as output from the computer system. The reader interested in these is referred again to the documentation for Statistics Canada's GIRLS (Hill 1981; Hill and Pring-Mill 1985, 1986).

Bibliography

This Handbook is written primarily as a guide for those who may actually be doing record linkage themselves. There are no references scattered throughout the account such as a scientist might expect. The Bibliography is restricted to a few of the journal papers and other publications dealing mainly with the practice or the theory of record linkage.

Acheson, E. D. (1967). *Medical record linkage.* Oxford University Press, London.

Acheson, E. D. (ed.) (1968). *Record linkage in medicine.* E. & S. Livingstone, Edinburgh.

Arellano, M. G., Petersen, G. R., Petitti, D. B., and Smith, R. E. (1984). The California Automated Mortality Linkage System (CAMLIS). *American Journal of Public Health*, **74**, 1324-30.

Baldwin, J. A., Acheson, E. D., and Graham, W. J. (eds.) (1987). *A textbook of medical record linkage.* Oxford University Press, Oxford.

Beebe, G. W. (1985). Why are epidemiologists interested in matching algorithms? In *Record linkage techniques — 1985: Proceedings of a workshop on exact matching methodologies*, Publication 1299 (2-86), pp. 139-44. Internal Revenue Service, Statistics of Income Division, Washington, DC.

Fellegi, I. P. and Sunter, A. B. (1969). A theory of record linkage. *Journal of the American Statistical Association*, **64**, 1183-210.

Hill, T. (1981). *Generalized Iterative Record Linkage System: GIRLS* (Glossary, Concepts, Strategy guide, User guide). Statistics Canada, Ottawa.

Hill, T. and Pring-Mill, F. (1985, 1986). *Generalized Iterative Record Linkage System: GIRLS*, (revised edn). Statistics Canada, Ottawa. [The Statistics Canada documentation of GIRLS is available from: Research and General Systems Subdivision, Systems Development Division, Room 2405, Main Building, Statistics Canada, Tunney's Pasture, Ottawa, Canada K1A 0T6.]

Howe, G. R. and Lindsay, J. (1981). A generalized iterative record linkage computer system for use in medical follow-up studies. *Computers and Biomedical Research*, **14**, 327-40.

Mi, M. P., Kagawa, J., and Earle, M. (1983). An operational approach to record linkage. *Methods of Information in Medicine*, **22**, 77-82.

Newcombe, H. B., Kennedy, J. M., Axford, S. J., and James, A. P. (1959). Automatic linkage of vital records. *Science*, **130**, 954-9.

Newcombe, H. B., Smith, M. E., Howe, G. R., Mingay, J., Strugnell, A., and Abbatt, J.D. (1983). Reliability of computerized versus manual death searches in a study of the health of Eldorado uranium workers. *Computers in Biology and Medicine*, **13**, 157–69.

Rogot, E., Feinleib, M., Ockay, K.A., Schwartz, S., Bilgrad, R., and Patterson, J. (1983). On the feasibility of linking census samples to the National Death Index for epidemiologic studies: a progress report. *American Journal of Public Health*, **73**, 1265–9.

Roos, L.L. and Nicol, J.P. (1983). Building individual histories with registries: a case study. *Medical Care*, **21**, 955–69.

Scheuren, F. and Oh, H.L. (1975). Fiddling around with nonmatches and mismatches. In *Proceedings, Social Statistics Section, American Statistical Association 1975*, pp. 627–33. Americal Statistical Association, Washington DC.

Smith, M.E. (1982). Development of a national record linkage program in Canada. In *Proceedings, Section on Survey Research Methods, American Statistical Association 1982*, pp. 303–8. American Statistical Association, Washington DC.

Smith, M.E. and Newcombe, H.B. (1982). Use of the Canadian Mortality Data base for epidemiological follow-up. *Canadian Journal of Public Health*, **73**, 39–46.

Tepping, B.J. (1968). A model for optimum linkage of records. *Journal of the American Statistical Association*, **63**, 1321–32.

Index